Jume Keith
Key West

More Postcards from Paradise

June Keith

Palm Island Press
Key West, Florida

D1360250

More Postcards From Paradise

Romancing Key West, Volume 2

By June Keith

Published by
PALM ISLAND PRESS
411 Truman Avenue, Key West, Florida 33040 U.S. A.

Library of Congress Cataloging-in-Publication Data
Keith, June
        More Postcards from Paradise : romancing Key West Volume 2 / June Keith.
        p. cm.
        Includes index.
        ISBN 0-9643434-0-1

        1. Key West (Fla.)—Social life and customs. 2. Key West (Fla.)—History. I.Title

F319.K4K45   1999   917.59'41   98-66398

This book is dedicated to Mikey Perez,
Miguel Norman Perez,
and Michael Keith,
with gratitude for the yin and yang of love
they have taught me to know.

TABLE OF CONTENTS

CONCH SALAD

CELEBRATIONS

TIES THAT BIND

*Topless dancing may not be the most wonderful job in
the world, but it sure beats hitting the road back to the mainland,
and former go-go girls always have titillating subject matter to
write books about.*

Paradise Junction

When my name recently appeared in a front-page newspaper story about topless dancing, a job from which I once eked my living in Key West, my editor said, "My wife was absolutely shocked to learn that you'd been a topless dancer. She thought you were a very respectable Key West lady."

Actually, I think I am a very respectable Key West lady. I thought that in 1974, when I came for a weekend visit and became hopelessly enamored with the place. I had a burning desire to stay, and a snowball's chance in hell of finding a job.

It's very difficult for newcomers to understand how barren the economic landscape was on this island 25 years ago. At the same time, the place was spectacularly alluring. The memory of that Key West, seen for the first time through my then raw and innocent eyes, keeps the dream alive. For many like me, abandoning the dream to move to the mainland for the comfort, respectability and predictability of back home can never be an option.

Back then, topless dancing at the Esquire Lounge was one of the only jobs available to girls in Paradise. When only $20 stood between me and that long drive back to the mainland, I signed on. For a girl who liked to party, dancing at the Esquire was a pretty good gig.

In the movie *Criss Cross*, a story set in '60s-era Key West, Goldie Hawn is a waitress struggling to support herself and her 12-year-old son. She wants to move into a nicer home than the seedy motel room she shares with her pubescent boy. But to get ahead in Key West, just as in real life, her only chance of improving her lot is to earn money dancing at the Esquire Lounge. One night Goldie's son follows her to work and discovers, to his horror, that his mom is a topless dancer.

In the film's final scene, after several hard-won lessons about greed, integrity and responsibility have been learned by both Goldie and her loving son, Goldie is seen pinning freshly laundered sheets on the clothesline in the sun-dappled yard of her clean, but modest trailer. She has achieved this domestic satisfaction with the money she's earned dancing topless at the Esquire Lounge. She has made concessions. Both she and her son now know that while topless dancing may not be the most wonderful job in the world, it's honest. And it sure beats hitting the road back to the mainland.

A 1975 documentary, *The Key West Picture Show* is another wonderful portrayal of the sultry Key West I encountered when I first landed here. I was working at the Esquire one night when two of my fellow dancers left early to get in on some action downtown. My sisters in go-go were invited to speak to the camera. They did, and their interview appears in the film.

"You have the freedom in Key West to express yourself as a dancer and as a person, too," Dancer Bobbie says, summing up the island's attitude in one neat verbal spin.

Life in Key West is challenging. It's difficult and spectacular at the same time. Fire and ice. We're here to test our souls' resiliency and to temper our strengths. Making a life in Key West is like running with the bulls. Shooting the rapids. Walking barefoot through burning coals.

Life in Paradise is bigger and better than real life. It's like the movies. The highs are higher. The lows are lower. And the people you know from year to year, season to season, day to day, are more vivid, more flexible, and more divine than most of the people you ever knew before. They are survivors, and their scars have made them beautiful.

Sometimes the balance between the surviving, and what we're surviving for, seems tenuous. So much about the island has changed. Great landmarks have been obliterated and important traditions have been diluted by Key West's brash success at tourism. Still, for as long as the sun shines in the clear blue sky overhead, Key West will remain a junction of Paradise and humanity, rife with contradiction and fresh challenge.

In moments of perfect balance, I am Goldie the go-go girl, sitting on the back steps of my little house, watching my snow-white sheets billowing in the bright sun, happy for the freedom to express myself as a dancer, and as a person, too.

STAYIN' ALIVE

Mick Martin

Key West or Bust!
After 22 summer vacations in Key West, our friend Thea finally
bought this little Conch house. She hopes to retire here someday.
Meanwhile, she spends each precious summer day she can in her Key
West retreat, and dreams of a year round future in Paradise.

81 Days in Paradise

This morning my summertime friend and neighbor Thea is waking up in a motel in Northern Florida. Today, she'll drive through Georgia, across the Carolinas and into Virginia. Tomorrow, she'll be home in her winter house, and on the day after Labor Day, back in her classroom, fresh and tan after 81 days in Paradise.

Thea's leaving has left me gloomy, just like when I was a kid and Labor Day meant I had to return to the prison of school. Nowadays, Labor Day means losing my girlfriend. When Thea's gone I won't have a pal who lives only a holler through my bathroom window away. I'll miss wandering with Thea through K-Mart on steamy afternoons when it's too hot to stay in the house. I'll miss having a woman my own age to talk to.

But she has to go. To spend 81 days here, Thea must spend 284 days in New Jersey, earning money. Yesterday morning, as I listened to the sound of her securing her house, slamming shut the trunk of her car, and pulling out of the driveway, I did not go to the door to wave goodbye.

Key West isn't a great place for people with abandonment issues. Everyone seems to be leaving, or preparing to leave, or working on finding a way to leave. There isn't enough money here, they say. It's too expensive. What — they haven't heard of brown rice and the Salvation Army Thrift Store?

As one who doesn't leave, I am privy to many confessions of disillusionment from those who could not find jobs, or stores selling Clinique beauty products, or a little Conch house to rent for under $1,000 a month.

A year or two down the road I am sure to hear from those same former Key West citizens, feeling nostalgic for the islands. They phone at odd hours, requesting updates on the activities of old lovers, bosses, and friends. They tell me about their air-conditioned jobs, fat salaries and benefits and their spacious homes. Then they ask if they can crash at my house for two weeks next winter.

Back in the mid-1980s I worked at City Hall in the office of Mayor Richard Heyman. The mayor received an unbelievable number of letters from people who'd heard of Key West and wanted information on how they might find jobs and homes here. Usually, we sent the classified section of the local paper and that would be the end of the matter. One guy offered to donate a kidney for the guarantee of a lifetime job and home in Key West.

When I waitressed on Duval Street I remember serving couples so sad little gray clouds were clearly visible over their heads.

"Tomorrow we go back home," they would explain. "But we're going to try to find a way to move down here permanently."

"What do you do?" I would ask.

"We're nuclear physicists," the answer might be.

"Ever waited on tables?"

Big laughter.

"I'll cry all winter missing Key West," Thea told my husband Michael the other day.

"Why don't you stay then?" he asked.

"How would I live?" Thea asked. "Teachers salaries here are half what they are at home."

"Yeah, but here we get paid in sunshine, and flowers and perfect weather," Michael said.

Last night as the nearly full moon rose, Michael and I went for a walk. We came upon a profoundly fragrant jasmine bush, so sweet my knees buckled. Michael picked a tiny blossom from the bush and held it to my nose, while I inhaled dramatically.

"Enjoy it, baby," he said. "That's this week's pay, plus your Labor Day bonus."

*Happy times in the waiters' station. My favorite bus boy and
adopted son, Nikki, (left) posing with waiter Jon Hynes
at the once-glorious, now gone, Lighthouse Cafe.*

Nikki Vicki Brenda

When he lived in Key West we called him Nikki Vicki Brenda. And because his mother is a writer, like me, and because we once figured that I really could be his mother, age-wise, he called me Mom or Mama.

For a few seasons we worked together at the Lighthouse Cafe. Nikki was a bus boy and I was a waitress. We had fun pretending to the customers that Nikki was my son.

"Mom," he would say beseechingly, holding a tray aloft in one hand, the other akimbo, "when you dressed me like a girl when I was little, didn't you think it might mess my head up just a little?"

To a table of obviously gay guys, Nikki might chat for a few minutes and then, with a perfectly straight face, say, "Gentlemen, where are the wives tonight?"

Nikki knew by heart every word of the script of *Female Trouble*, the kooky John Waters film.

"I got a knife in my purse," he would hiss into my ear, as I tried to get an order from a table of grumpy tourists. "And I'm going to cut you up after work!"

It's a line from *Female Trouble*.

Nikki Vicki Brenda had not only a remarkable talent for comedy, but a magnificent voice, too. He mimicked Whitney Houston or Diana Ross perfectly. He danced. He whirled. He sang into a restaurant pepper mill as though it was a microphone. Then, just when his audience was truly mesmerized, he would stop, blush, and laugh self-consciously.

He told me that he'd tried to perform in a variety show in high school. But he'd lost his nerve, and rushed off the stage before he even got started. He sang in church when he was very young. He'd been an altar boy, too, in his hometown of Homestead, Florida.

In Key West, Nikki spent many hours volunteering at AIDS Help and Helpline. But he rarely mentioned his volunteer work. He rarely talked about anything serious. He was too busy making people laugh.

One of Nikki's two brothers was shot to death in Miami. The other is an officer in the Air Force, like his dad. His mother is a devout Christian. His parents have been divorced for a long time.

Nikki's family is loving, and supportive, but they have difficulty understanding his quirky genius. It's hard to watch someone with so much talent, so much intelligence, always fooling, ever the clown.

Eventually Nikki left Key West to live with his mother in Marianna, Florida. We exchanged letters. Nikki was a good writer, too. Insightful. Crazy. Hilarious. Heartbreaking.

"It's hard for me to get off the couch," he wrote a year after he left. "Things are going down the tubes for me healthwise."

It was the first time he'd mentioned to me that he was ill, though I knew.

"I have everything I could ask for here, but friends," he wrote. "Your letters make me so happy!"

I wrote a story about Nikki in the paper. I described what a great, funny, caring person he was, how much he'd given to Key West, how sick he'd become, and how hungry he was for mail.

After that Nikki was besieged with letters and cards from well-wishers, some of whom had never even met him. He was thrilled with the outpouring of compassion and his new pen pals, who kept him busy for the final six months of his life.

"Mama," he wrote in his last letter to me, "you know how much I love you! If you don't then one more hug can't hurt."

Susan Pitts

There are more ghosts than just Hemingway's hovering near
this landmark. This wall of red brick surrounding the Hemingway
house was built in 1935 by Pauline Hemingway's childhood friend,
Toby Bruce. Toby came from Piggott, Arkansas to construct it. He
married a Key West woman and lived here with her until he died.
Their son, Dink, lives on the island still.

The Great Wall

I t is rare for a day to pass when I am not asked for directions to the Hemingway House, which is located four doors down the street from my own.

The path to Hemingway's House has been beaten quite smooth by now. You would think the location of the town's most famous tourist attraction would be anything but a mystery, and yet, nearly every time I exit my home I am approached by people who ask in tentative tones, "Is this the way to the Hemingway House?"

We are so close to the place I could almost yell to Larry Harvey, my very debonair, snowy-haired friend who works the ticket booth there, "Hey Larry, how are you today?" And he could sing back, "I'm fine, darling! How are you?" And we would each hear the other.

Once I was hired to write a brochure for an English

painter named Patricia Townsend who moonlighted as a tour guide at the Hemingway House. I invited her over for dinner, at which time I hoped to get to know her better.

"Can you come at six?" I asked.

"Yes, if the damned tourists don't keep me late asking ridiculous questions about the great Hemingway," she said scornfully.

"What kinds of questions?" I asked.

"Obnoxious ones. They want to know: 'Is this where he shot himself?' and 'Is this where he went to the bathroom?' They're disgusting!"

"So we'll see you around six?" I asked.

"Yes. All right. But tell me, what do you eat? No meat, I hope."

"No," I assured her. "No meat. I'll fix pasta."

"With tomato sauce?" she asked. (She pronounced it toe-mah-toe.)

"Yes, and lots of garlic," I said. "We love garlic. It discourages the mosquitoes from biting us."

"Oh, I can't have garlic! It will carry on my breath when I give tours to the Hemingway fans," she said.

"Fine. No garlic," I said.

"You don't have any animals do you?" she asked.

"No." I said.

"Because I hate the way you Americans go on about your house pets. People go mad for those mangy Hemingway cats. They pick them up and kiss their little faces! I find it utterly appalling!"

"No animals," I said. "But we do have a little boy. Do you like children?"

"Ab-hoooooor them," she said, turning her head as if avoiding a bad smell.

"Oh, I see. Well, perhaps we'd better postpone this visit until my son grows up and goes away to college," I said.

In fact, I never did write that brochure. And Patricia Townsend, who'd hoped to find happiness and artistic success in Key West, was ultimately very disappointed here. Her next move was to Indiana, and that's where she died.

Still, I can't help remembering her feisty spirit when I pass by the Hemingway House. The other day, I was walking by the great brick wall that surrounds the place. I thought of Patricia Townsend, and I also thought of Toby Bruce. Bruce was a childhood friend of Pauline Hemingway's who came all the way from Piggott, Arkansas to build that brick fence. Toby loved Key West. He married a Key West woman, and they lived here for the rest of their lives. Their son, Dink Bruce, lives here still.

"Is Hemingway's house around here?" a woman anxiously asked, breaking into my thoughts.

"It's right here," I said, patting Toby's handiwork. "Right behind this wall that Hemingway had built to keep out the tourists."

Ann L. Williams

*One morning a blind chicken flew into my head,
causing me to drop two plates of banana pancakes into
the dirt. Customers laughed. The cook was furious.
And I thought to myself: how did a nice girl like me end up
in bacon and egg Hell? It was my last day of waitressing.*

Hell At Blue Heaven

Waitressing, they say, is like riding a bike. Once you learn how to do it, you don't ever forget. So, after a two-year sabbatical from waitressing, with Christmas shopping season fast approaching, I went in search of a position as a food and beverage server.

In spite of advice from wise, former waitroning friends who warned that the breakfast shift in any eatery is a sure route to bacon-and-egg Hell, when I was offered a job working the day shift at the famous Blue Heaven, I signed on. Breakfast from 8 a.m. till noon. Lunch till 3. All of it served outdoors in a garden beneath ancient hardwood trees.

Ricky's Blue Heaven Restaurant is located in a busy junction of earthy local color, at the corner of Thomas and Petronia streets in Bahama Village. The old neighborhood, with its friendly dogs, happy children, painted bicycles and nonstop action, is the kind of place that people without firsthand knowledge imagine all of Key West to be. Heartily praised in print by venerable travel journalist, Charles Kuralt and recommended regularly in travel guides, the Blue Heaven has become a must-see on every adventurous tourist's itinerary.

Blue Heaven customers are happy campers from the moment the host shows them to their painted table. Here is what they've been searching for! Atmosphere. Charm. Funky-looking island people. Cats. And live chickens.

"The cats don't bother the chickens?" customers ask.

"Who owns these chickens?" some want to know.

"Where do these chickens sleep?" a lady asks. "Where do they lay their eggs?"

After a lengthy exchange that is a necessary part of every breakfast order — how do you want your eggs cooked? Potatoes or grits? Ham or bacon? Multi-grain or rye toast? Pancakes or banana bread? — there is little time for chicken chat. Little time for anything else at all except to fly into the kitchen, place the order, pray the cook is in a good mood, and dash back out again to refill empty coffee cups and run for more butter, or cream or syrup.

After my first eight-and-a-half-hour day of waitressing, just before I fell asleep around 8 p.m., my husband and I fondly recalled the bygone days of ninety-nine cent breakfasts at the Fourth of July Restaurant on White Street. Breakfast was Cuban toast slathered in butter, a slab of salty ham, grits and two eggs. The waitress never dreamed of asking how you wanted your eggs. Oh, you could request over-easy or scrambled or sunnyside up. But everybody's eggs came out the same. Fried. Who would argue over ninety-nine cent eggs?

Customers of the '90s warn, don't break the yolks or I won't eat them.

After a week of working at Blue Heaven, influenced by my fellow workers' blue nail polish, beads and dreadlocks, and their nonchalant approach to shaving, I began to feel the need for some body-piercing, or at least, an exotic tattoo. I described this longing to Cynthia, a trendy-looking kitchen worker, and the following day she brought me a batch of *Skin and Ink* magazines, from which I might find ways to fashion a trendier me.

My fellow servers at the Blue Heaven, clear-eyed beauties in Zen-decadent garb, are predominantly young. There is a reason for this. Only the very young can handle the breakfast shift with its inherent challenges and detail-laden script. A farsighted baby boomer, with fading audio powers and a memory like Swiss cheese, is no match for the eggs-over-easy-or-else crowd.

And so, after three weeks and twelve breakfast shifts at the Blue Heaven, I bade farewell to my server sisters, Samantha, Renata, Vanessa, Melissa, and canceled my appointment with the tattoo artist.

Michael Keith

*Vic Dunn holds court in a favorite corner of his screen-walled
living room. To his right, a can of beer; to his left, a bottle of mosquito
repellent. Vic told us that he liked living on his own private island
just fine. His wife, however, was growing tired of the dampness and
the commute to work. She was ready for a less-rustic home, with modern
conveniences like flushing toilets, running water and nearby grocery stores.*

Little Knock 'em Down Key

Rocky, my adventurous brother who lives in New York and dreams of living in the Keys, telephoned the other night. He's come into some money and is looking to buy himself a little piece of Paradise. He called to say he thinks he may have found it in the classified pages of a Keys newspaper.

"It's on an island ten minutes from Summerland Key," Rocky said. "A place with a funny name. You need a boat to get there. Will you check it out for me? Find out where they go to the bathroom."

It made sense that Rocky would be intrigued by visions of life on a tropical island far from the hustle and bustle of tourist-swamped Key West. His New York home is on a remote and woody tract, miles of backcountry roads from civilization.

Rain fell heavily from low, dark clouds on the Saturday morning my husband Michael and I were scheduled to see Little Knock 'em Down Key. Just before we left our house in Key West, the real estate agent, Richard Coarse, phoned to advise us to wear sneakers and long pants. He said he hoped we wouldn't mind "getting a little bit wet."

It didn't seem like a good day for boating, but, encouraged by Richard's enthusiasm, we headed out into the downpour. The rain stopped and the sun began to appear by the time we found the Galley Grill on Summerland Key and waited by the door for our ride out to the island.

Had we launched from the other side of Summerland, explained our navigator Vic Dunn, it really would have taken only 10 minutes to get out to Little Knock 'em Down, just like the ad said. But we were taking the long way around, which meant we motored through a mile or so of canals before we reached the open ocean. Either way, the cost of hiring Dunn's flat-bottomed skiff for the round-trip to tour the island property was $25.

"You eliminate a lot of curiosity seekers that way," Coarse explained, as we climbed out of the skiff and onto the island. The tide was low, so we didn't get wet after all.

The quiet on Little Knock 'em Down Key was velvety soft. Almost eerie. Dunn, our navigator, turned out to be the owner of the place. He's 68 years old, and has lived on the island for 18 years. He'd live there longer were it not for his wife's growing disenchantment with island dwelling.

He hastened to add that she had been a darn good sport all these years. The house, with its screened walls and odd collection of mix-and-match furniture, was neat as a pin, something like a well-organized campsite. In the kitchen, pots and pans hung neatly from a shelf over a kitchen sink, into which the only available water came from huge plastic barrels of collected rain water.

Through the years, Dunn said, he'd dreamed up lots of ways of making the place more cushy, but somehow he'd never gotten around to most of them. A bigger generator would be nice. The 3,600-watt generator there now makes too much noise. But big generators require lots of gas, he said, and he didn't like the idea of paying for, or hauling, all the fuel it would require.

"What about plumbing?" I asked, as we sat in a sitting room and watched brilliantly colored birds darting in and out of a feeder a few feet away.

"Why? Do you have to go?" Dunn asked. "There's a bucket right outside the back door if you do."

"What about the cold?" Michael asked, warily eying the walls of screen. "It must get cold out here in the winter. "

"Sure it does," Dunn said, chuckling. "You layer lots of clothes on when it's cold."

Living on an island, he said, is a lot like living on a farm. There are many chores to do. The life ain't easy, but it will keep a man in shape, Dunn said.

"Say you need a piece of parsley for cooking," he said. "You've got to get yourself ashore, go to a store, buy what you need, get it back to the boat, motor it back out to the island, walk it up to the house. And that's before you even begin to use it."

Dunn's place, on the market for two months now, is a turnkey sale. Everything you see on the island stays on the island. Even the cats, who darted off like wild animals at the sight of us.

"They're not used to seeing anyone else around here but my wife and me," Dunn explained.

The tide had risen by the time we headed back down the path to the boat. We soaked our shoes, and the bottoms of our jeans. We laughed a lot on the way back to Summerland, imagining how it might be to live out there.

"So what do I tell Rocky?" I asked Michael, as we headed back to Key West.

"Ask him if he wants to go halves on the place," Michael said.

*How do Nashville songwriters Chuck Krumel and Michael Keith
keep those smiles plastered on their faces in the feast or famine world
of country music? Living in Paradise helps a lot.
The goofy hats help, too.*

Overnight Success

L ong before I knew him, my husband Michael read that if there was something he really wanted to do he should write it down on a slip of paper and keep it in his wallet so that whenever he opened it, he would be reminded. As a businessman, homeowner and father of three, he opened his wallet quite often in the next ten years, and every time he did, he saw that slip of paper. "Write songs" it said.

Years later, after his fortune had changed, and many years after he'd put it there, he opened his wallet and read that little slip of paper for the ten-thousandth time. And that time, something clicked. He began to write songs.

That was around the time when I met Michael. I felt pretty awful when he told me that he wrote country songs. I didn't like country music. I mean I really didn't like it. So my heart sank when I learned of Michael's dedication to that particular genre.

One summer night we laid together on the beach beneath a clear, warm sky waiting for shooting stars. Michael sang "Talk To Me," a soft, sweet song from the '50s, and told me how he'd heard it for the first time on his father's car radio in South Carolina, on a very starry night just like this one.

Then we saw a shooting star. That night we pledged our love, and I said a silent prayer that our extremely dissimilar tastes in music would not one day become our undoing.

Do you have any idea what it's like to live with a songwriter? It's like this: Michael roams the house at night, humming tunes and mumbling rhymes. He jots down bits of verses on yellow legal pads that are stashed into every nook and cranny of our home. When anybody says anything funny, or cute, Michael will say "Hey! That's a hook!" which means that you may be hearing your words as the chorus of a song a few weeks hence.

He gets frisky when I wear cowgirl boots.

When it is time to write songs, all other activity in our home must cease while the living room is taken over by Michael and his Key West writing partner, Chuck Krumel. Chuck plays guitar, smokes cigarettes and drinks coffee. Michael hums and croons and slurps endless glasses of iced tea. I stay out of their way.

Michael has songwriting partners in Nashville, too — cowboy types who know where the best meat-and-two-vegetable joints are, and regularly bump guitars with people like Reba and Garth.

We've even considered moving to Nashville for a while, so Michael could work full-time on his songwriting. Once we packed up my son Mikey, then 11 years old, and took him to Nashville for a look-see. He began to throw up about an hour after we got to the motel. He didn't stop vomiting until we were on our way back to Key West three days later.

So much for moving the family to Nashville.

Considering the competition, the chances of a musically untrained, former-businessman dreamer writing a marketable song are obviously quite slim. And yet Michael has done it. Two years ago we celebrated the arrival of Michael's first royalty check. It was for a song written in Nashville in 1989, recorded in Australia in 1991, and released there in 1993.

A year-and-a-half ago the group Perfect Stranger released an album with a song by Michael on it. Later, the song was released as a single, with a slick video. The song is "I'm A Stranger Here Myself." He wrote it in Nashville 5 years ago. The album, for a while in music stores everywhere, was Michael's first bona fide shot at the big time. What a thrill!
Nowadays we're back in the waiting mode.

The myth of flash-in-the-pan success is just that: a myth. In the past 12 years Michael Keith has written over 300 songs, and suffered the same amount of rejections. His ability to remain optimistic in spite of all that is inspiring. And contagious.

"If I can do it, you can, too," is Michael's message.

Believe it!

Susan Pitts

Former high school football star, father and businessman
Ben Pitts demonstrates his winning ways with luggage and
baby-making on the front steps of his Birmingham home.

You Can't Get There From Here

I t was love that brought Ben Pitts to Key West. He followed his college sweetheart, Susan Jones, here. Susan was a fun-loving cheerleader two years younger. Ben was a serious student. They met at South Carolina's Presbyterian College. A record-smashing high school athlete with both athletic and academic scholarships, Ben excelled in business school, easily earning his degree a couple of years after they met.

To Susan's chagrin, Ben began his first job as a manager in a textile mill, only two days after graduation. Susan had envisioned a long, lazy celebratory holiday to mark the occasion.

While Ben worked a swing shift at the factory, Susan stayed in school. But the stress of Ben's crazy hours and Susan's growing disinterest in attending the college where her boyfriend, the former big man on campus was no longer present, created discord in their relationship.

Susan left for the Southernmost point, where she found an apartment, a job, and a prime spot on Sands Beach. She sent Ben letters full of funny stories of her sub-tropical adventures, in envelopes thick with photos of her beach-babe self, blond and very tan.

When he could bear the separation no longer, Ben quit his job and came to Key West, where he was quickly frustrated by the lack of management jobs available on the island.

"He was too ambitious for Key West," Susan says.

Susan's goal was Paradise, and she'd found it. She worked on her tan by day and earned astonishing tips serving cocktails in the Havana Docks Bar at the Pier House by night. She fell in with a bunch of like-minded island girls. By the time Ben showed up, Susan was plugged into an active party loop.

One night Ben was hanging around waiting for Susan to finish her shift when he heard that a bellman had quit. Desperate for gainful employment, he took the job.

"A bellman only has to know two things," Ben said. "One: the location of the ice machine. Two: how to find the rooms. It's not a difficult job."

During his 3-month stint as a Pier House bellman, Ben escorted several famous Margots to their rooms: Margot Kidder, who radiated star quality, and Margot Hemingway, who did not.

"She seemed needy and sort of lost," Ben recalls.

Ben's best weekend was when the International Boat Races came to town. That Saturday his tip take was almost on a par with Susan's.

With his terrific good looks — he's a ringer for the young Rock Hudson — and his easy Southern charm, Ben made a fine bellman. So fine that several guests sent letters to the Pier House commending the obviously over-qualified young man on his winning demeanor.

When the Pier House sales manager left, Ben saw his window of opportunity. He applied for the job, but he did not get it. Discouraged, he headed home to launch what is today a stellar career in marketing.

Susan eventually got her fill of Paradise and married Ben. Today their Birmingham home is filled with Key West-themed books, paintings, and T-shirts. And amid the jumble, two kids. When she has time to think about it, what she misses most about Key West, Susan says, is not the parties or the night life. It is the clacking sound of palm boughs in the breeze.

Ben admits that he sometimes wonders what might have happened, how their fate might have been altered, had he landed that job at the Pier House. But those thoughts are rare. A man on his way to the top doesn't have time to reminisce.

Skipper Kripitz

Happy Birthday, Mo! A cool party on the deck behind Louie's Backyard, circa 1980. From Danny Simpson's scrapbook. Danny is the bearded guy, seated on the far right, front row. Mo is also on the front row, the second girl down from Danny.

We're Cool

Thank God for John Kiraly's Big Amana. Three years ago, the world-renowned painter of fantasy and light decided that his industrial strength cooling unit, though chillingly efficient, was too noisy for his painting studio. Who would argue with John Kiraly?

"Do you know anyone who wants a big, cold air conditioner like this?" John asked us one day. "I've ordered a new, quieter one."

A week later, John's rejected Amana was cooling every room in our little house just as well as we imagined central air conditioning might, if only we could afford it.

My husband was not as grateful for our good fortune as I. He felt that the big, noisy air conditioner was evidence of how soft we'd grown. To him, relying on air conditioning is somehow perverse; non-organic. He's intrigued with the idea of roughing it in Paradise. Robinson Crusoe is his hero. But I am no Friday.

Ten years ago we went through summer without any air conditioning at all. I swear I don't know how we did it. The only explanation I can offer is that we were very, very much in love then, very young, and very forgiving. Today, we'd survive for about 20 minutes without the Big Amana.

By way of bemoaning progress and the cost of air conditioning, Michael likes to tell the story of his erstwhile fellow trolley driver Richard Barnes, who, in the mid-'80s, was the first driver to buy an air conditioner for his home.

"The first hurdle was to buy it," Michael recalls. "Then, you had to pay to run the damn thing."

"I figure it will cost me a dollar a day," Richard told his shocked and envious co-workers. "But I don't care. It's worth it."

"We thought he was living like a mad king," Michael says.

Musician Danny Simpson remembers that in the old days, before air conditioning was generally affordable, islanders stayed cool by spending as many hours as possible out of doors. Summertime beaches were much more crowded then, and Key Westers had more leisure time to spend on them.

Sturdy window fans were popular then, too. They were cheap, and a good one did double duty. In addition to keeping the air moving, it kept out nighttime noises.

"Give me the very loudest window fan you've got," Danny remembers telling the salesman at Sears. "I live in a very noisy neighborhood."

In the last ten years I've watched with satisfaction as the air conditioned age has sneaked up on us. It started with little air conditioners in the bedrooms. Then came Kiraly's Big Amana, which was originally switched on after lunch, but only on the the hottest summer afternoons. Then it came on in the morning, and stayed on till after sundown. Now, we turn it on before we make the coffee, and turn it off after the 11 o'clock news. In a week or two it will go on, and stay on...till late fall.

Last year we discovered that City Electric will average out a year's worth of electric bills, both big and small, and send one medium-sized bill every month. A revelation!

Hey, we're economizing! Crank it up!

Alan Maltz

*"Giving and Taking" is the name of this photograph
by Alan Maltz. It appears in his book,* Key West Color.
*Too bad our friends lost their copy before they got to see it,
and to contemplate its message.*

The Sting

The last time my brother Rocky, who lives in New York, came to the Keys to do some fishing he brought along a buddy, Joe.

Naturally, Joe fell in love with Key West. Ever since that visit, Joe's been planning his retirement in Paradise. Once in a while he phones to ask a question about something or other, and we're always happy to answer it. Joe's a nice fellow and we certainly understand his passion for the island. When it was time for Joe to get married, he decided to bring his fiance here to tie the knot.

Sarah doesn't fish, but she likes to shop, and she was definitely ready to get married. In Key West. Or anywhere. Even before she'd been to the Keys, she agreed to retire here with Joe someday. She's pretty much willing to do wherever Joe asks her to do.

Rocky was invited to the wedding, but he wasn't too anxious to come here during the heat of summer. So when the Joe and Sarah wedding party, which consisted of Joe and Sarah, arrived in town, they phoned us. They were in a prenuptial daze, all goofy and excited. Joe invited us to go with them to dinner that night, but my husband Michael and I had recently decided to eliminate dining out from our routine as a cost-saving measure. Instead of going out for expensive meals, we decided we would buy expensive ingredients, stay home, and have our feasts our way.

"I'll cook dinner," I said to Joe, on the phone. "Come to our house and I'll fix you a welcome-to-Key West feast."

I prepared Conch fritters. Peel-and-eat shrimp. Key lime pie with fresh-squeezed limes. And at every course, lots of stories and laughter about the vicissitudes of life in the tropics.

Sarah asked where we thought they should have their wedding dinner. She named a few places, but said that they were pretty set on Louie's Backyard.

"Whaddaya think?" Sarah asked. "Is the food good?"

"It's good and the place is beautiful," I said. "But it's awfully expensive."

"It's our wedding dinner," Sarah said. "We don't care what it costs."

"So go to Louie's," I said. "Bon appetit."

I was feeling pretty pleased with myself as I cleaned up the monstrous mess I'd made, creating my local-color food sampler. We'd avoided a big dining out dent in our budget, and fulfilled our social obligations to my brother's fishing buddy and his fiance. We'd wished them a happy life, and sent them on their way.

The next day, Joe called to invite us to the wedding dinner. Another couple from New York had flown in for the wedding, and they would be at the party, too. Yes, it would be at Louie's, because they wanted it to be great. And they really, really wanted us to be there.

Louie's? We bought Alan Maltz's spectacular $50 coffee table book, *Key West Color*. What a way to remember a Key West wedding. What a way to say "thanks for taking us to dinner at the most expensive restaurant in town."

The newest members of the party, a couple named Jack and Tina, battled throughout the wedding dinner about a misunderstanding they'd had at the Miami Airport hours earlier.

"Do you see what you're signing on for, Joe?" Jack said, while his wife cursed all men for making all women miserable.

"It starts in Catholic school, when you keep us dumb and ugly in stupid uniforms and clodhopper shoes," his wife Tina said bitterly.

Over dessert and coffee, which Joe insisted we should all order, I thanked God that I'd escaped from New York. Then the bill came and Joe and Sarah came out of their love cloud and studiously examined it.

"June and Michael don't drink, so they only owe $100," Joe said.

I choked on my decaf and Michael handed over his credit card.

The next day Joe phoned us from the airport.

"Time for the long ride home," he said regretfully.

"Take the Alan Maltz book on the plane with you," I said. "It's very entertaining."

"Yeah. I can't believe Sarah left it under her chair at Sloppy Joe's last night!" Joe said. "Hey, maybe you can get another one and send it to us?"

"Yeah, maybe," I said. "Hey, bon voyage and have a good life!"

My friend Garth Bandell, all these years after his illustrious career in musical theater, displays his show-stopping good looks in the jungle paradise of his back yard.

Peep Show

A few weeks ago my son Mikey was home from school for Spring Break. On the first night he was here I went into his room to tuck him into bed. We were chatting softly when the late night quiet was shattered by the lonely midnight crow of a wild rooster.

"Oh Mama," he said happily, "I'm know I'm home when I hear that — the sound of my Key West."

The confused chickens of Old Town cockadoodledoo at all hours of the day and night, and also seem to have no sense whatsoever when it comes to getting to the other side of the street. Down here, we are accustomed to stopping our cars to let mama hens and their peeping chicks cross.

Visitors to the island seem enchanted by our flock of lost and unclaimed birdbrains. Many times at the Blue Heaven Restaurant I've seen tourists carefully photographing roosters as if they were some exotic tropical species. They feed them bits of bread and ask staff questions about where the chickens nest, sleep and lay their eggs.

But not everyone is as charmed as our tourists and my Conch son by these runaway yardbirds. Many of our Old Town neighbors complain bitterly that the noisy roosters keep them awake too many nights. And I have a friend whose mother, brought up on a farm in Tennessee, wouldn't stay for lunch at Blue Heaven because she didn't want to eat in a yard with chickens scratching at her feet. No matter how good the food.

My husband Michael and I celebrate special events with fried chicken dinners at the Deli Restaurant. It's actually become a tradition for us. Any good news around here calls for Deli Restaurant fried chicken.

Michael phones ahead to the kitchen and says, to whoever answers, "Ask the cook to drop a couple fried chickens for Michael, would you please? We'll be there in 20 minutes." He says it as if he knows all about the politics of the short order kitchen, when in fact, all he knows for sure is that fried chicken takes a while to fix. He likes to arrive at the Deli right when his chicken's coming out of the fat, find a seat, select two from the veggies of the day list, decide between a biscuit or corn muffin, and get down to business.

It's one of those Key West insider's secrets he's proud to know.

I remember the day my Nova Scotia uncle invited my cousins and me into the barnyard to watch him slaughter a chicken for our dinner. I have been intimately hip ever since to the meaning of the term "like a chicken with its head cut off."

My friend Garth, who lives on a quiet-as-a-Tennessee-farm lane in Old Town, told me that his peace was recently disturbed when a rooster took up residence beneath the house next door to his. The bird crowed from dusk till dawn keeping Garth and his neighbors awake night after night.

In desperation Garth posted a handmade sign on a telephone pole offering $100 reward to whoever could rid the lane of its raucous rooster.

The chicken posse arrived in the form of a mother, a father, and two young sons. The mother knocked on Garth's door and asked if the reward was still available. It was. With deep skepticism, Garth indicated to the family the location of the rooster's hide-out beneath a neighbor's house.

The boys jumped out of the car with a chicken of their own. They placed it on the ground within view of the renegade rooster. Within seconds, Garth's lonely lane bird came out from under the house to investigate. With that the little boys scooped up the birds, one each, and jumped back into their car. The entire procedure had taken minutes.

Garth gave the mother the money and the family drove away with the fruit of the day's labors: chicken dinner and a hundred bucks.

Michael Keith

*Crazy like a fox. Artist and visionary Ann Labriola designed
and created* Stargazer, *the world's largest (50,000 pounds!)
underwater sculpture.*

Ann Labriola's Nuts

These are wild and crazy days at the Nut House, a nut and dried fruit emporium on Big Coppitt Key. Christmas shoppers are buying pounds of Keys Crunch, a bark-like brittle of nuts, seeds and honey, Duval Crawl, spicy Chinese crackers, and bags of golden-yellow dried mango. They're buying Scorned Woman Hot Sauce and Bloody Mary Mix, and handcrafted trays shaped like lizards, fish, and shells.

At the center of this sea of fast commerce and holiday cheer, owner Ann Labriola is busy at a counter, wrapping gift trays of gourmet goodies for shipment to Bloomingdales, Saks, and a slew of other fancy food boutiques. As she works, Labriola chats easily, laughs often, and answers many questions. All the while, her hands, ever graceful and sure, are moving.

There is an art to all of this, and in fact, she is an artist. Labriola is a renowned sculptor, whose monumental works have brought her fame, but not fortune. Making a living in the pricey paradise of the Florida Keys is an ever constant challenge.

She never really expected to make money on her sculpture, Labriola says, and she never has. In the twenty years since she arrived in Key West, with a masters degree in fine arts from the San Francisco Art Institute, she has cleaned houses, maintained yards, waited tables, and developed photographs in a home darkroom to pay the bills.

She has also created several colossal sculptures, all designed to promote her artistic vision: the union of art, nature and archaeology. Her most notable work, *Stargazer*, is the largest underwater sculpture in the world. It is two-hundred-feet long, seventy-feet wide, ten-feet high, and wrought of 50,000 pounds of steel. Holes on *Stargazer*'s surface form patterns of star constellations. Resting on a sandy bottom, in 22 feet of clear, blue water, *Stargazer* is 5 miles from Key West, pointing due southwest toward the Sand Key Lighthouse.

In the three-and-a-half years since it was anchored to the ocean floor, nature has turned it into a magnificent ecosystem, encrusted with a stunning variety of marine organisms, and swarming with brilliantly colored fish. It is a favorite diving spot, and an amazing sight when viewed from the air on a full moon night, outlined in phosphorescent sea life. *Stargazer* has become precisely what Labriola created it to be — a living link between sea and sky.

The project took three years and $125,000 to complete. Labriola raised most of the money herself. Sunny and warm, her demeanor combines equal parts of blithe charm and earthy intelligence. Once she wore knee pads and knelt before gallery owner and Key West Mayor Richard Heyman to beg for money. He wrote her a check for $500.

"I'm used to people looking at me as if I'm crazy," Labriola says, shrugging. "But it takes a lot to give something lasting to the world."

Labriola, 41, grew up in a close-knit Italian family in

Armonk, New York. Her father owned a landscaping business. A brother, now dead of AIDS, was an artist. Her mother, 78-year-old Rose, is also a sculptor, who still spends long hours each day at her art.

After the holidays, when her business is back on an even keel, Labriola will devote herself fully to her latest project already in the works. A scale model of *Journey Through Time in a Galaxy*, a sculpture and artificial reef to be anchored off Miami's South Beach, has been exhibited and enthusiastically received by the Miami art community, as well as Dade County environmentalists.

At more than 10 times the size and mass of *Stargazer*, *Galaxy* is Labriola's most formidable project yet. It will cost $550,000. Fund raising goes into high gear when all the permits are in place.

Meanwhile, Labriola the businesswoman works 14 hours a day, socking away money for the lean times ahead, when she switches back into her artist's mode.

"The way things are going," Labriola grins, "It doesn't look like I'll be getting out of the Nut House till after Christmas."

Heritage House collection

*The poet who read at John F. Kennedy's inauguration,
shown here with his Key West landlady and hostess
extraodinaire, Jessie Porter.*

Working 9 to 5

My brother Rocky, who lives in New York, phoned the other night to ask me why I hadn't called him lately.

"I got a job." I told him. "I work all day."

"Oh man," Rocky said, heaving a big sigh. "All day? That's rough."

"And when I get home," I said, "I'm usually too tired to start talking on the phone."

Rocky has a job, too. He's a garbage man. He starts picking up trash before dawn. By noon he's home, with the rest of the day for himself.

"Why don't you get up real early and go to work," Rocky suggested. "It's nice a quiet at 5 a.m. Nobody's around to bother you."

"They pretty much want me to be at my desk from nine till five," I explained.

"All day?" Rocky said again, in disbelief.

A few nights later Rocky called again.

"Did you get your schedule straightened out at work yet?" he asked.

I recounted this conversation to my pal Dilys, who owns Miss Marbles Parlour, a mystery book shop. Dilys is also founder of Murder Ink, the famous New York City book store. In New York, Dilys says, finding people to mind her shop was very easy. She'd run an ad and job applicants would show up wearing suits and offering impressive resumes.

But here in Key West folks do not seem to be seeking steady employment. Here, Dilys never finds anyone willing to keep shop for a full day. When people respond to her ads for help, she knows better than to ask anyone to work from 10 a.m. all the way through till 6 p.m.

"So I ask them what hours they would like to work," Dilys explains. "If they say they'll work from noon until 3, I say fine, and I do my errands between noon and 3."

My mother worked as a night nurse for her most of her adult life, which made her crazy as a loon, but free in the daytime to handle her affairs. Once she decided to try working the day shift, and was astonished at how inconvenient a day job is.

"When do people who work all day go to the bank?" she implored. "When do they go to the post office or the grocery store?"

When our 17-year-old son Mikey came home from school for Christmas vacation, I suggested that he work a few nights at Friday's, where he worked last summer, to pick up some extra money.

"That's the craziest thing I ever heard!" Mikey said.

"Why is that so crazy?" I asked.

"Think about it, Mom," Mikey said. "I'm home for Christmas vacation and you want me to work? If you wanted me to work, why'd you send me a plane ticket to come home for vacation?"

And it was Mikey who explained to me why the poet Robert Frost, who reportedly wintered in Key West for 18 years, never wrote a poem about the island.

"He was on vacation," Mikey says. "He wrote his New England poems, the ones that made him famous, in the summers when he was up North. He came down here to party."

Mikey, who moved to Gainesville, Fla. in July, has had difficulty finding work there, although he job hunts regularly. Last fall, potential employers asked him if he planned to go home for Thanksgiving and Christmas. He dutifully confessed that he did. So, he was not hired. After the holidays, however, he remains unemployed. Recently I asked him exactly what he says in job interviews.

"I say that I'm a student and I want a part-time job a couple of evenings a week, with Friday and Saturday nights off," Mikey said. "Then I tell them I'm a Conch, because people really love it when you're from Key West."

Michael Keith

David: How about taking one shower a day out, too?

June - Arriving soon ! Hope you can put me up for a few days. Can stay no more than a week. You won't need to cook much as I eat usually a meal a day out. Regards to hubby. David S.

David Who?

It is March 1 and we citizens of Key West are about to become very, very popular! We can expect to hear from old friends, many of whom have remained out of touch since last year at just about this time. Former classmates, lost lovers, and far-flung relatives are about to contact us with big news. It is this: they're coming to Key West! To see you and me!

Like this guy David S., whoever the hell he is.

There is a famous Ring Lardner short story called *Haircut* in which a traveling salesman with a perverse sense of humor picks random names off of mailboxes and, just before leaving a town, sends suggestive messages on postcards to the Mrs. of the house. I would like to think that this postcard of mine is the work of such a prankster.

But I think that something far more sinister is going on. I

think someone named David S., who I can't for the life of me identify, really is coming for a week-long visit. David S., whoever he is, will have to wrestle with my mother, my brother Rocky and his fishing buddy, and Michael's cousin John-Dewey for sleeping accommodations which, in my house, consist of one very tired futon and a non-sleeper style sofa.

There is a Buddhist expression that says that there is no such thing as a home too small for one more guest. Only a heart. I've got news for the Buddhist who said that. My house, which unbelievably once housed a Cuban cigarmaker's family of 7, really is smaller than my own heart. Much, much smaller. My heart, I figure, is around the size of an acre. My house, I know, is 800 square feet.

It is difficult for those who live in sprawling New England or Canadian Maritime houses, like most of my kin do, to imagine our abbreviated version of domesticity here in the American sub-tropics. Even my poorest relatives at the far tip of Nova Scotia have automatic dish-washers and a couple of extra beds and a space heater in the barn to accommodate occasional visitors. When I tell them we have no such luxuries here, I suspect they believe I am fibbing to discourage their visits.

My mystery house guest, David S., indicates in his communique that I won't need to cook much during his stay, as he "takes at least one of his meals out each day." Where did he get the idea that I cook regular meals, or any meals at all? This faceless friend does not know me very well...

In reading between the lines of this postcard from David S. I suspect there will be requirements not listed. He sounds suspiciously like one of those guys who claims to be getting away from it all, but never really is. I've had this kind of guest before. They beg us to keep the phone lines clear while they await urgent news from the coast, nervously anticipate Faxes and regularly bust into my writing time to check their E-mail on the computer.

He'll probably expect to find a free parking space.

The best kind of company are the folks who leave on bicycles first thing in the morning, and return late at night, fed, entertained and tired. In my experience, those independent types are rare. More often, guests expect you to join them in their relentless dedication to tourism. They beg to be accompanied on Duval Street shopping sprees and trolley tours. They pummel you with questions and keep you up late. Go to bed at your customary and workaday time of 10 p.m. and they accuse you of party pooping.

David S., if you're out there, please reconsider. After all, we really do not know each other well. Not anymore, anyway.

Gail Brockway

Don't cry for me, Argentina. We're doing just fine. Ray
is a registered nurse now, gainfully employed at the local
hospital. Dougie is back in Sante Fe. The new owners of
the Lighthouse Cafe who wanted to replace the old staff with
a new one are gone, too…and so is the Lighthouse Cafe.

Ray Gets Fired

When my friend Ray phoned last night, I sensed a scary edge in his voice. I thought he might be calling to tell me that someone had died. I tensed as I waited for the bad news.

"I just got fired," he said, his voice quivering. "I got fired — over the phone."

I met Ray six years ago when I worked as a service bartender at the Lighthouse Cafe. Ray was a waiter. He was quiet, sweet and sexy in a dark, smoldering sort of way I found irresistible.

"You remind me of the Italian boys I used to run with back home," I teased him. "Whenever I get homesick for New York, I'll call you."

Ray has been working in restaurants since he was 15 and lied about his age to work in a fast-food hamburger joint in

Cleveland, Ohio. He's always dreamed of becoming a nurse. But first he wanted to get his house finished, and save up the money to pay for nursing school.

After a year of bartending at the Lighthouse Cafe, I was promoted to the wait staff. Ray trained me and remained my mentor throughout my 5-year waitressing career.

Ray always worked hard. While most waitrons goofed off pretty regularly, he stayed in constant motion. He was a detail man, who made certain at the beginning of each shift that we had enough napkins folded and enough lemons cut. Sometimes his dedication was almost irritating. "You'd think he owned the place," we'd gripe. Actually, his devotion was vital. Someone had to care the way Raymond did.

On his twelfth anniversary with his lover Ron, Ray couldn't get the night off. So Ron came in for dinner. After I'd stopped at Ron's table to chat, an older lady at the next table asked, "Is that nice young man a friend of yours?"

"Yes," I answered. "He's celebrating his anniversary tonight."

Later, when he had a few minutes, Ray sat down to drink a glass of champagne with Ron.

"It's too bad that man's wife couldn't be with him on their anniversary." the woman sighed. "Where is his wife?"

"Oh, that's his partner," I said, pointing to Ray. "I mean they're not married exactly, but they've been sharing their lives for 12 years! Isn't it wonderful?"

The woman looked confused for an instant, as she sorted through the information. Then her face softened and she smiled.

"Yes, it is wonderful," she said.

Eventually, the Lighthouse Cafe was taken over by new owners, a couple who were new to Key West and island ways. Many longtime staff members split. But Ray, finally enrolled in nursing school, stayed. And so did I. Eventually we two were the only old-timers left. Then, a couple of weeks ago I quit. And last night, Ray was fired.

"We're going with an all new staff this season," he was told.

For a hardworking person like Ray to be fired from a job he's held for ten years is a terrible shock. My heart ached for him when he told me. I love Ray a lot, and I felt how bad he was hurting.

Ray will be all right. He'll find another job to sustain him as he goes through nursing school. As employees go, he's a catch.

"You've seen a lot of changes over the years, haven't you?" people remark upon hearing I've been living here for 20 years.

Yes, I've seen changes. But the hardest changes aren't necessarily the ones you can see. Some of the scariest changes are the ones you feel. The face of Key West is changing, but so is the heart and the soul.

Little Stevie Dufresne

*Jon Hynes and me on one of a thousand nights we shared
working at the Lighthouse Cafe. This night was Fantasy Fest.
The theme was "Jungle Madness." See the whip around my neck?
I was decked out as a wild animal trainer, which describes the job
of waitressing in a busy Key West restaurant on any night,
not just Fantasy Fest Eve.*

It's Always Later Than You Think

My friend Jon Hynes prides himself on his ability to pack everything he needs for interstate travel into a small duffel bag and to be ready to hit the road at a moment's notice. For many summers he has worked as a roadie for rock bands. He digs being on the road. He loves seeing America from the driver's seat.

Jon has maintained a great little apartment in Key West for a dozen years. But he is finding less and less need for a home these days since his road gigs are becoming more frequent. This summer, while he was on the road with the Rolling Stones, he sublet his apartment.

Jon came back into town at Christmas time. He's driving a cab these days, a job he sincerely enjoys. He loves sharing his sunny disposition and his vast knowledge of Key West with visitors to the island.

Even when he's here, we don't see much of Jon. He has a busy social life, and enjoys spending time alone, too. But he phones, and his news is always fascinating.

"Let me tell you about the crazy week I just had!" Jon said during a call yesterday. "I decided to take the HIV test. If it was positive, I decided I would move into my apartment full-time and settle here. If the test was negative, I thought I would give up my apartment and settle into a really nice place in New Orleans — because it's cheaper there, and New Orleans is more centrally located. Then I'd just visit Key West when I could."

I was surprised at the news. Jon, like many people I know, has always been vehemently opposed to seeking out his HIV status. He lives a very clean life. He is a vegetarian who consumes little fat and sugar. He quit smoking years ago. He goes to the gym regularly. He is a picture of good health; robust, sober and enthusiastic.

"What changed your mind?" I asked him.

"About Key West?" he asked.

"No, about taking the HIV test," I said.

"Oh, I needed the information to settle my future," Jon said. "But there's more. My landlord called me yesterday to tell me that he has sold the building! My apartment is gone!"

"What a bummer!" I cried.

"Yeah," John said, "But all I could think of when he told me was, thank God. Now I don't have to take that damn HIV test."

"I'm glad you're not taking it," I said.

"But I am going to take it," Jon said. "I decided I want to know."

"Hey, we all want to know if some fatal disease will hit us someday," I said. "But there is no test we can take to guarantee whether or not we'll be sick or well five or ten or fifteen years from now."

"But for me, there is," Jon said simply.

At a memorial service for my friend Conrad, someone

talked about how having AIDS had given Conrad's previously undirected life a sure focus. Preparing for his death, his transformation, became Conrad's brilliant career. When he died, he died gracefully and self-actualized, a hero for our times.

Many people who discovered themselves to be HIV-positive a decade or more ago have lived thus far feeling just as well physically as they ever did. Who's to say when and even if they'll succumb at all?

What changes when the HIV-positive alarm clangs, is the way people live with it. They learn to treat themselves, and those around them, better. To nurture their bodies and their spirits. To open their eyes and their hearts to others, and learn to recognize the river of humanity that runs through each of us — sometimes in a weak trickle, sometimes in a mad, gorging stream.

I don't think Jon Hynes could do life any better than he does it already. He is a model of mental and spiritual good health. He lives as if his HIV test already came back positive. Maybe we should all live that way, because ultimately, we're all positively going to die.

ROCK STARS

Capt. Tony collection

*Father of the bride: Captain Tony in the doorway of
Captain Tony's Saloon, on the occasion of his daughter
Coral's wedding, which was staged in the bar and celebrated
in the pool room.*

"Our lives change like weather, but a Legend never dies."
Jimmy Buffet, "Last Mango in Paris"

Last Mango in Paris

W hat do you call him, I wonder, as we knock on his door. He's been Captain Tony since he arrived on the island the 1950s and captained a charterboat. He owned and operated Captain Tony's Saloon, where, he wistfully recalls, he once watched literary lords Tennessee Williams and Truman Capote ballroom dancing together "like a couple of grandmothers." He was mayor of Key West during some of the island city's most golden glory days. *The New York Times* dubbed him the Salt of Key West.

He's even come back from the dead. A few years ago, he suffered a massive heart attack, and was whisked away from the local hospital in the middle of the night to be ambulanced to a Miami for heart surgery. The following morning, when his fellow patients saw his bed and his room empty, they speculated that Captain Tony had not made it through the night. A rumor that he had died swept across the island like a wildfire. But two weeks later he was back in town, with a repaired heart and a new episode to laugh about — his own death.

Captain Tony's life story is currently being adapted to the big screen in Hollywood. There is a sizzling biography in the works. A pretty young woman answers the Captain's door. Between hugs, handshakes and introductions, you find yourself with a big, happy grin on your face. And speechless. The 80-year-old captain beams as he rises from his chair to greet his guests. He moves his ashtray from the table to the floor, explaining, "I have one bad habit only. I smoke."

He introduces his wife Marty, the lady who answered the door. She is a third her husband's age, pretty and prim as a schoolteacher. Several kids appear, the youngest of the 13 he has fathered in his life. ("So far," he likes to joke.) The little boy and teenage girl ease gracefully into the background as their famous father holds court at the kitchen table.

There are scrapbooks piled high on the table. I've come to borrow some photographs. But before we get down to business, Captain Tony schmoozes a bit. He tells us how great we look, and teases my husband Michael about coping so gracefully with being married to me, "a member of the opposite sex."

"Remember the time when everybody thought you'd died from the heart attack?" I ask him.

"Yes," he says, smiling. "A lot of people in Key West still think I'm dead."

A couple of weeks ago, when Planet Hollywood opened a restaurant in Key West amid great publicity and a big, invitations-only bash, featuring movie stars and local celebrities, Captain Tony was not on the guest list.

"I probably wouldn't have gone anyway," he grins ruefully. "I don't like crowds much, and if I'm not the center of attention, I don't really want to be there."

He's smiling, but it's clear he's hurt by the slight. It's not that he minds missing another party. He's partied enough for two more lifetimes. It's just that he's done so much for Key West's image. He's a living legend, the guy Jimmy Buffett wrote about in the song, "Last Mango In Paris." Jimmy even used to fly Captain Tony to his concerts, seat him in the audience, and introduce him to the Parrot Heads just before he sang "Last Mango."

How could Planet Hollywood not know that having a party in Key West and not inviting Captain Tony is like having a mass and not inviting the priest?

When we get to the scrapbooks, we pause frequently to look and listen while Tony tells the story that goes with the picture. They are good stories of old Key West.

There's a picture of Tony and two daughters posing with a 1400-pound tiger shark on Garrison Bight. The teeth from that same shark, Tony tells us, are on exhibit at the Smithsonian Institution. There's a picture of Tony in a tuxedo, smoking a cigarette in the doorway of Captain Tony's Saloon, as he awaits the arrival of his daughter Coral on her wedding day. Photos from *The Wall Street Journal. The New York Times. People Magazine. The Miami Herald.*

The stories keep coming. Marty fixes coffee. The beautiful daughter wanders into the kitchen for some breakfast.

"I'd like to find a nice young man for my daughter there," Captain Tony says, his famous baggy blue eyes twinkling. "If he can give me a pig and two sheep, he can have her."

Heritage House collection

*An ageless portrait of writer Jeane Porter, a Key West native
who grew up at 410 Caroline Street in what is now the
Heritage House Museum. Jeane's famous mother
entertained American luminaries like Robert Frost,
Tennessee Williams, Tallulah Bankhead, Sally Rand
and Mr. and Mrs. Ernest Hemingway.*

Born Of The Sun

The Hemingway myth that attracts millions of tourists to his house is much bigger than the true story of Hemingway in Key West. People like imagining him as a burly macho-man, swaggering through the streets of Key West drunk and smelling of fish, a bully and a lout, who stomped women's hearts and punched the nose of anyone who got in his way. There are seeds of truth here, but those who knew Ernest Hemingway in Key West tell a far different story.

Hemingway was a man of exotic tastes. He loved Spain and all things Spanish. Key West in the 1930s was still very much a Spanish-influenced place. Imagine the delicious fragrance of suppertime black beans permeating the air he breathed as he walked up Whitehead Street to his home after an afternoon of fishing or drinking in the local color at Sloppy Joe's.

Jeane Porter remembers Pauline Hemingway's devotion to

her important husband and the fine, comfortable home she kept for him. Jeane grew up in Key West, in a house a few blocks down Whitehead Street from the Hemingways. In the '30s, she was often a guest there. Jeane, a tomboy who shunned dolls and preferred running and climbing trees to tea parties, grew up playing in the spacious garden with the Hemingway boys.

Yes, Jeane recalls, Hemingway was a restless man. But a kind one. And a great one. This they all understood. When Jeane's father first met Hemingway, he observed: "He appears to breathe more air than most people."

Artist Mario Sanchez and his wife Rose lived in a little Conch house across the street from the Hemingways. Mario, who still lives and works on the island, remembers that Hemingway sometimes came over in the late afternoon, after a day at sea, to offer the young couple fish from the day's catch. Mario gratefully accepted the grouper and snapper, and politely turned down the sailfish.

Yes, Mario has heard the stories of the Hemingway myth, the stories of the bully and the drunk, but he can't support any of them. The Hemingway he knew was a gentleman and a good neighbor.

To set the record straight on Hemingway in Key West, as well as a number of other famous people and places from the island's history, Jeane Porter has written a memoir. In *Conch Smiles* she writes of many anecdotes involving the Hemingway kids and Pauline Hemingway.

Photographs of Pauline don't do her justice, Jeane Porter says. Pauline was very attractive, small-boned, thin and androgynous. She wore her hair short, and dressed in slacks or shorts. She was an excellent fisherwoman and hunter, taught by her famously outdoorsy husband.

In Jeane Porter's written recollections, Pauline Hemingway emerges as an unsung heroine: the good, supportive woman behind the great man. Because Jeane was actually there, and remained friendly with Pauline after her divorce from Hemingway and until her death, her impressions ring sweet and true.

"Hemingway had this magical quality, this charm about him, that touched everything and everyone. He gave off light," Jeane recalls. "Yet he was no polo player; no snob. He was larger than life. We in Key West owe him a debt of gratitude. I hope we don't drown it in a flood of beer and crud and greed."

In describing Hemingway's brilliant effect on those around him, Jeane evokes a line from a poem by Stephen Spender, "I Think Continually of Those Who are Great."

"Born of the sun they traveled a short while toward the sun, and left the vivid air singed with their honour."

*Author David Kaufelt and artist Betsy Minter acting
in one of Dilys Winn's wacky whodunit dramas at
Miss Marble's Parlor and Book Shop.*

We'll Die For You

After watching a couple friends perform in a campy, interactive whodunit parlor game at Miss Marble's Parlor and Mystery Book Shop, I suggested to shop owner Dilys Winn that if she ever needed a big blond, I was available. Her bright eyes, aglow with a glimmer of lunacy, turned neon when I said my husband would act, too.

Finally, our chance came. Last week Dilys called and asked us to appear in one of her zany dramas. I would play a whorish psychic. Michael would be a nerdy IRS agent. Were two roles ever so clearly ours? All we had to do, Dilys explained, was enter the parlor at 8 p.m., clutch our throats, stagger like poisoned people dying hideous deaths might do, and — die. Easy enough.

"Sure," I told Dilys. "We'll die for you."

Dilys sent me to the Knot So New Consignment Shop

where Ilene, the shop owner, who really is psychic, handed me dress after whorish dress to try, while a salesgirl named Lucy and I discussed the meaning of the word "whore." Does a whore get paid a lot for sex, or simply have a lot of sex? I say the second. Please don't ask me why.

After I'd found my costume, a tight green and gold skirt with a giant flounce in a shimmery fabric, with a matching leopard-skin print jacket, I was to report to Dilys for costume approval.

"Here are my corpses now," Dilys said to someone on the other end of the phone, when Michael and I walked into her shop.

Dilys loved my costume, and was so encouraged by our enthusiasm for acting, she made an impulsive decision to expand our roles. After our death scenes, according to the new script, we were to quickly change into angels' wings and choir robes. Oblivious to anyone else but our ghostly selves, Michael and I were to wander around, discussing bright white lights at the end of a tunnel. We were also to drop occasional clues.

Late Friday afternoon, while I teased my hair and applied a half pound of make-up, Michael hunted for the gray flannel suit he'd stashed in the back of his closet 10 years ago. While he knotted his tie, I parted his hair down the middle and plastered it with gel. We found his old briefcase.

At 7:30, we headed on foot for the mystery theater, with absolutely no clue of how our appearance on Duval Street would affect sunset pedestrians. Michael, the nerd in the suit and tie carrying a briefcase, and I, his whorish companion in the leopard skin suit, jangley jewelry and cheap perfume, created a bona fide scene.

"Is this your first blind date?" I shrilled to Michael as we passed a group of pedestrians. Some polite types tried hard to not stare. Others glared at me disapprovingly.

"How do you like Key West so far?" I shouted gaily, as

Michael managed to stay in poker-faced character.

A girl sitting on the sidewalk stared hard, and then when we were past, sighed loudly and gasped "My nerves," as if she'd hallucinated us.

Soon, it was 8 o'clock. Showtime! As we waited in the wings, with the other, more seasoned cast members, Dilys appeared to give us some last minute directions.

"When you do your death scenes, really camp them up," she said to us. "You should really overact, and don't worry about looking foolish. "

Then, as a sort of afterthought, Dilys murmured, "I could never do what you're about to do."

But Michael and I had no qualms about looking foolish, and no fears of losing our dignity. Our impromptu dress rehearsal on Duval Street had cured us of all that.

A pretty portrait of gentle Nancy, creator of a magnificent acre of rainforest in the heart of Old Town Key West.

Nancy's Secret Garden

Since the story of Nancy's Secret Garden appeared in the best-selling book *Charles Kuralt's America*, people have been coming to the garden to take her picture, ask for her autograph, and converse with the lady whose huge vision is far greater than the sum of her parts.

Through the nearly thirty years she's been on the island, a persistent rumor has followed Nancy Forrester. Maybe you've heard it. The word is that Nancy's loaded. Rich. Independent. It's just a rumor, mind you. But it seems that the rumor keeps folks from understanding how she, with the magnificent acre of rainforest in the heart of Old Town Key West, might be suffering financial woes.

"I am from a wealthy family," Nancy admits. "Before my generation, no one in my family worked for what they had. They inherited it."

She inherited money too, but she spent it, traveling the world, and then, on the ramshackle Conch house and chunk of land that has become Nancy's Secret Garden, the place Charles

Kuralt wrote about.

"My mother worked before she met my father, and understood the value of the work ethic," Nancy explains. "She worried that I wouldn't learn that myself."

This rainforest is Nancy's career, a work of art in progress, the artist's life work. Like all gardens, it is never done, and it never will be. There are no photographs to show what it looked like when Nancy arrived decades ago. Then, the property was a dumping ground for old appliances and garbage. Vagrants slept beneath its one original tree, an ancient gumbo limbo. Thousands of dollars have gone into the purchase of the many trees and plants that flourish here today. In terms of blood, sweat and tears, the tally is inestimable.

Tending Nancy's Secret Garden, with it's many species of palms, two thousand orchids, and plots of exotic flowers, is a back-breaking job. The garden must be watered, pruned and fertilized. Nancy's has become a last refuge for parrots whose owners no longer want to keep them. The birds arrive in elaborate cages, some speaking, some not. Nancy does not turn any bird away, and her rainforest bird community has grown along with everything else in the garden.

Obviously, Nancy cannot handle the work alone. She depends heavily upon volunteers who are willing to do any chore for the privilege of spending time in the garden. During the winter tourist season, when the town is packed and many visitors pay $6 each to see Nancy's astonishing masterpiece, she takes in enough money to pay a gardener. But he leaves the island every May. And even if he didn't, there is no money for his salary in the summer.

Money also comes from the rental on a little cottage that she leases out to honeymooners and others who appreciate its rustic chic. When it rains, refunds are in order. The tin roof leaks, and there is no money in sight to repair it.

The garden is a favorite place for weddings and memorial

services. Ashes have been scattered here. For these reasons and more, it is a sacred place, as sacred as an Indian burial ground, Nancy says.

Sometimes when her funds fall critically low, Nancy asks the local media to help by publishing stories about the garden, urging the townspeople to buy memberships. $50 a year for a couple, and not much more for a family seems a good deal. But rather than eliciting memberships, such press often attracts people interested in making her spectacular offers and deals. This frustrates and confuses Nancy. She needs money to see her through the crucial summer months.

She is 58 years old now and her hips and back often ache from her labors. Sometimes she cries from fear. But the garden is her legacy, the plants and trees are her children, and she cannot surrender without a hard fight. How does she tell those who would buy her out and send her packing with a pocket full of money, that she doesn't want to sell her children? She only wants what all mothers want: to see her children grow and prosper. To see them survive beyond her.

"If only my mother could see what I've worked to create here," Nancy says, "she would be so proud."

Gotham Studios, NYC

*That's playwright Arthur Miller (top) sharing a ladder
with producer Frank Taylor (far left). By the time this photo
was taken, Miller's marriage to Marilyn Monroe was over, and
in spite of the Hollywood smiles, no one else on the famous set
was having a very good time either.*

The Misfit

K ey West publisher Frank Taylor says he doesn't like to talk about his Marilyn Monroe days. But he will, from time to time, offer up more clues to the mystery of America's most glamorous icon.

The adventure started one summer day in 1958, when Taylor's friend, playwright Arthur Miller, invited him to visit his home in Roxbury, Connecticut.

"Bring the kids," Miller suggested.

So Taylor loaded his four sons into the car and drove from New York City to the country house Miller shared with his famous wife, Marilyn Monroe. When they arrived, the playwright read aloud the first draft of a screenplay called *The Misfits*.

As Miller read, the drone of a vacuum cleaner, and the bumping, scraping sounds of housekeeping came from the second floor above them. Finally, the cleaning noises stopped. And then, a moment Taylor and his sons will never forget: Marilyn Monroe, her hair tied back, her face make-up free, lightly bounded down the stairs and into the room.

"She was a very pretty girl," Taylor says, and his eyes sparkle.

"Miller wrote *The Misfits* for Marilyn," Taylor explains. "She had said every line in the play. *The Misfits* is a true evocation of her beauty, her sensitivity, and her care for animals. I think she cared for animals more than she did for people."

At Marilyn's behest, Taylor became producer of *The Misfits*. At the beginning of their collaboration, Marilyn Monroe and Frank Taylor were great friends, deeply appreciative of each other's special qualities. But sadly, by the time the filming was done their relationship had crumbled. And so had her marriage to Arthur Miller.

So what was Marilyn Monroe really like?

"Marilyn had a need to seduce every man she met. Emotionally. Psychologically. Physically," Taylor explains. "She would unload her sad, ugly background on anyone she met, right at the beginning. She played on the sympathy of every person she encountered."

"She'd had a horrendous childhood. She really played on the waif thing. She made everyone feel protective of her. That's why women loved her, too."

But once she'd finished exposing her unhappy past, Taylor remembers, she got back to the business of being a movie star. She was an expert at it, a consummate professional. She took her job very seriously.

"She never appeared in public without make-up," Taylor says. "She did not have great legs, but she had great shoes, very high heels that made her legs look great. She changed her clothes at least five times a day. She couldn't bear the thought of disappointing her public."

Frank describes how Marilyn studied anatomy and knew how to pose her body at its very best. Every one of her gestures, every move she made, was studied, rehearsed. The way Marilyn walked, sat, rose, and disembarked from a plane, was practiced.

The way she tilted her pelvis, bent her ankle, carried her spine and ribs, all spoke of her understanding of her own physique.

"She wasn't showing off," Taylor explains. "She was being a star. She delivered."

As he reminisces, Frank Taylor's admiration of Marilyn Monroe is obvious. Evident too, is his sadness — vague, shapeless, but unmistakable.

"I loved her," he says finally. "All men did."

So why couldn't America's most dazzling star find happiness? Why could no one save her?

"She had no self-esteem at all," Taylor says. "It was the problem with all her relationships. They foundered on the fact that she felt she was not a worthy person, or even a good actress. Eventually that lack of self-worth transferred from her to you. It poisoned everything."

"But oh, when you were with her," Frank says softly, "she made you feel like a prince."

The Fabulous Spectrelles. What woman wouldn't kill to be
transformed for just one night into a sloe-eyed doll with the kind of
behind that the designers had in mind when they invented Spandex?

Walking In The Sand

The other day I was at my girlfriend Sally O'Boyle's house, waiting while she tended to her rambunctious little 4 and 5-year-old boys, when I spotted a teasing comb and a jumbo-sized can of Final Net hair spray on the dining room table.

"Girlfriend!" I said. "I didn't know you teased your hair. I thought that snarl was an accident."

"Oh, I haven't told you yet," Sally laughed, tossing her regally red head. "I'm a Fabulous Spectrelle now! I tease my hair into a big beehive every night!"

I almost fainted with envy.

"Can I try your false eyelashes?" I asked weakly. "Is it fun being a Spectrelle?"

"It's the best fun in the world," Sally said, grinning as if it was 1966 and we were getting away with something big.

If there really is such a thing as reincarnation, I want to live my next life in the body of a narrow-kneed girl with a great voice and big hair. The next me will look terrific in eye-liner,

harmonize like an angel and sashay with the nonchalance of a
Brooklyn slut. I will sing back-up doo wop in spiked heels, and,
because I will never even think of trying for lead, every other girl
in the group will be my friend.

Just a mention of the Fabulous Spectrelles, Key West's own
retro girl group, and the fantasy center in my brain is off and
running, churning vampish visions to the rhythms of doo ron
ron. And I'm not the only one. I know dozens of women on this
island who would gladly give up their off-street parking places to
spend a night crooning and shaking their booties with the
Fabulous Spectrelles. Who wouldn't kill to be transformed, just
for one night, into a sloe-eyed doll with the kind of behind that
the designers had in mind when they invented Spandex?

Being a Spectrelle answers Sally's lifelong dream of being
on stage. Performing, and foraging for the next opportunity to
perform, up until recently has been the prime focus of her life.
In a way that perhaps only other performers can really
understand, my friend Sally is most alive, her truest self, in front
of an audience.

"I always wanted to be a big star," Sally says. "I wanted to
marry Sean Penn and have an apartment in New York and a
house in L.A."

Eight years ago she went to New York for one final shot at
fame. For a year she concentrated on doing nothing but
whatever it would take to land a role in a Broadway show, or a
Hollywood film. But no part materialized. And in the course of
giving it her all, she realized that she was no longer willing to
devote her life to the tantalizing and ever-frustrating pursuit of
stardom. She wanted something different, something surer.

"Today I'm married to a middle-aged Republican with a
job," she laughs. "He's not Sean Penn, but…he's Mr. Right.
Marriage and children have changed my life in ways I'd never
imagined would happen to me."

Still, she says, there's this need for the spotlight that will never go away. It's a pleasure button in her personality that can only be punched by performing. From time to time, there's a role in a play, or a temporary singing gig — like this one with the Spectrelles — and the actress/singer inside of her gets a life-affirming dose of validation.

"The other day I told my husband, 'you know how good you feel when your golf score is 80? That's how I feel when I'm on stage with the Spectrelles singing 'Walking in the Sand.' "

When Sally, daytime mother and real estate broker, nighttime doo ron diva, dons her pantyhose, big hair, eye-liner, false eyelashes, and her '60s-era dresses, her little boys watch in fascination. They run their hands over her legs encased in nylon and they giggle.

"Oh Mom, you're so cool," they tell her, and Sally's heart bursts with a different kind of happiness.

"Performing used to be my everything," Sally says. "Now it's the icing on the lovely cake that is my life."

Eileen Bridges

*The King's Southernmost Fan Club, the Snorkeling Elvises.
The 100% polyester, practically indestructible Elvis jumpsuit
is suitable for snorkeling, partying, parading, or changing
the oil in your pickup truck.*

A Little Bit of Elvis

Elvis impersonator Otis May, founder of the king's southernmost fan club, says he now knows why Elvis Presley wore sunglasses at night.

"People are snapping your picture all the time when you're Elvis," May says. "Flashes are constantly going off in your face."

"We must have been photographed at least 300 times last night," Valerie May says. "And downtown was actually pretty dead last night."

The Mays call the phenomenon "the Elvis thing."

It all began a few years ago when the Mays dressed up as Elvis and Priscilla for Fantasy Fest. Before the Elvis thing, thanks to Otis' costume dealer cousin in Memphis and their own inventiveness, the Mays had won lots of prizes for their fantastic costumes.

But nothing in their masquerading past had prepared them for the amazing and unabashed adulation heaped upon them when they took to the streets as the king of rock 'n roll and his dark-eyed queen.

"People want to touch you. To give you money. To carry your guitar case," says Otis May. "You've never felt anything like it."

Today in Key West, there are around 13 Elvis impersonators and roughly the same number of Priscillas. They call themselves the Snorkeling Elvises, inspired by the Parachuting Elvises portrayed in the movie *Honeymoon in Vegas*. The Snorkeling Elvises Fan Club is one of 250 officially sanctioned by Graceland. Their local charity (all Elvis fan clubs must have one) is the Monroe County Association of Retarded Citizens.

In addition to sponsoring an annual Blue Hawaii Beach Party fundraiser for the MARC group home, the Snorkeling Elvises appear frequently at local events. They arrive in a pink Cadillac.

Sometimes a group of Elvises in white, gold-studded jumpsuits don scuba equipment and descend 25 feet to participate in the annual Underwater Music Festival at the Looe Key National Marine Sanctuary. Photographs of the Snorkeling Elvises appear in newspapers all over the world.

The official Snorkeling Elvis jumpsuit costs $250, but it's practically indestructible, and includes the Elvis wig and sideburns. The suit is polyester which means it's hot. Yes, you sweat a lot, but it's also wash-and-wear.

"You can wear it snorkeling, partying, in long parades, and even to change the oil in your pickup truck," Otis May says.

Priscilla's costume calls for a $50 foot-high beehive wig, lots of '60s era eye make-up, a pastel mini-dress and high heels.

"Every Priscilla's hair has to be the way Elvis wanted it to be," Valerie May explains. "Elvis designed her hairstyle and her black eye-liner. She had to wear that eye-liner at all times — even when she went into the hospital to give birth to Lisa."

The Mays visit Otis' hometown of Memphis every August 17, the anniversary of Elvis's death. They pay homage to the King's memory at Graceland where they mix and meet with thousands of fellow Elvis fans who spend that day there, too, to remember and compare lives.

"When I tell people I'm originally from Memphis, they say 'You mean you lived this close to Graceland and you moved away?' They just can't believe any Elvis fan would chose to leave Memphis," Otis says.

Every Fantasy Fest a bigger crowd of Otis May's old Memphis pals buy Elvis costumes from his cousin, and come down to Key West to be Snorkeling Elvises.

"Sometimes they're a little reluctant to try it," Otis May explains. "But the new Elvises always tell us it's the most fun they've ever had."

Same for the Priscillas, says Key West real estate agent Debra Benedict, an ardent Priscilla impersonator.

"Of course we Priscillas are just satellites. The Elvises are the big thing," Benedict says. "But until you put on that Priscilla wig you cannot even begin to imagine how incredible the Elvis thing is! Even as a Priscilla, you become part of something much bigger than yourself."

"What makes the Elvis thing so great is that you instantly become a celebrity. You can know what it's really like," explains Otis May. "You put the costume on and instantly, you're a huge star. Take the costume off and you're you again."

"We're careful not to over-expose this thing," he says. "We only need to do it once in a while — 'cause a little bit of Elvis goes a long, long way."

*Key West's own divine Miss M. A girl who never,
ever held back anything.*

The Divine Miss Merle

When guys at the topless bar ask Merle for her age, the 47-year-old exotic dancer tells them she's 100. When you know Merle, and love her deeply the way her friends and I do, she doesn't look 47 or 100 or 35. She doesn't look any age at all. But Merle's no liar. Heart and soul-wise, she really is 100.

She grew up in Westchester County, the darling daughter of middle-class Jews. Beautiful, bright and with a voice that could knock the Harlem Valley local out of Grand Central off its tracks, Merle was singing professionally before she was out of elementary school, and exhibiting the darker side of child stardom, too. She was also fussy, unhappy, and tantrum-prone. She sang jingles, demo records, and, just into puberty, could mimic perfectly the voice of her idol, Aretha Franklin.

When Merle was 21 she was singing back-up on a demo record for a then-unknown pianist named Barry Manilow. Another singer named Melissa Manchester was there. And Gail Cantor. Barry invited them to audition for a new up-and-comer named Bette Midler. Midler had recently appeared on the *Johnny Carson Show,* where she'd wowed Johnny and his audience. Now she was preparing for a concert at Carnegie Hall.

"Sure we went," Merle says. "And we got the job."

An intense schedule of rehearsal followed. After practice the trio would go for tea, and Merle, who liked Bette, but was unimpressed with her singing, would whisper to her pals "This girl is nothing without us!"

When Bette's Carnegie Hall debut came, all that changed. Merle was shocked to see Midler, "a girl like any other," step onto the stage and metamorphose into a shining diva. It was a breathtaking revelation.

"In rehearsals she saved voice," Merle explains today. "She knew what she could do. She knew that she didn't have to knock herself out for us at rehearsal."

It was an eye-opening experience for Merle, a woman who never, ever held back anything. She went on the road with the Divine Miss M when her baby boy was past 3. By the time her son was 10, Merle's voice had begun to slip alarmingly.

She consulted every known doctor and therapist in the East. Acupuncture. Throat doctors. Holistic centers. Her search led her to consider her health, both mental and physical, in a new way. She become a devotee of aerobics, and then body-building, and all of that gave her power and self-respect.

"I was in my 30's before I took my first happy breath on this earth," she says.

Then, tragedy. Merle's beloved son died, at age 22, in a drug experiment gone fatally off course. Her only child's father, whom she hadn't seen in many years, was at the funeral. The parents reunited, and Merle moved from NY to South Florida with her former husband.

The reunion didn't take, and soon she was out on her own again, searching for work. On a cruiseship, singing back-up for

Lesley Gore, her voice finally crashed and she realized that her singing career was over.

"I'd lost my son," Merle says. "I'd lost my voice. I'd lost myself."

She was teaching aerobics, drowning her suffering with lots of drinking, when a guy friend took her to a topless club in Homestead. "You could do this," he said. There was a woman on stage, dancing naked. "I could never, ever do that," she said.

Two days later, her career in exotic dancing began. And that's what she's doing still, sans the drinking and the self-pity. She likes her job.

"My family raised me to be a hard-working and responsible performer," she says. "That's what they expect of me."

Every week Merle attends 2 butt-shaping classes; 2 abdominal flattening classes; 3 to 4 hard aerobic classes, 5 or 6 hours of bicycling or stair climbing, and 3 supervised weight sessions with a trainer. Lately she's on a mission to locate a plastic surgeon.

She meditates, explores her psyche, reads and studies. She shops in secondhand stores and makes art of zen-decadent fashion. She pumps herself up in every way she knows how.

"With our outsides we portray how we want to be perceived by the world," Merle explains. "I want my appearance to say I'm strong and powerful. Because inside, of course, I'm frightened."

And beautiful. Inside and out.

White Trash Night at the Savannah Restaurant. Garth is the highway trooper. His partner, Billy, is the cook with the fly swatter. Savannah was famous for its funky staff, and its down home Southern cooking.

Full Moon, Full Circle

T he nearly full moon appeared on the horizon when my
friend Ann and I set out for a walk. The day had been
long and busy for both of us. The cool, fresh evening air
was deeply restorative. Soon we found ourselves on Olivia
Street beside the cemetery, and then on a tiny lane.

"I know someone who lives here in an incredibly neat
house," I said. At the house I called his name through the
screen door.

Garth invited us in and led Ann on a tour of his cozy and
rustic retreat. She was clearly charmed. In the back yard Garth
invited me to feel the water in a small, coral rock-lined pond. I
knelt down and dipped my hand into the pool. The water was
silky and warm as a bath.

"Oooooooh," I said. "I want to go in."

"Me, too," said Ann. "Can we?"

"Sure," Garth said. "I'll turn on the jacuzzi jets. But I have
only one ladies' bathing suit."

"No problem. We're no ladies," we quickly assured him, as

we stripped out of our clothes and eased ourselves into the jacuzzi/pool.

The water was warm and dark and friendly as a womb. After we jacuzzied, we swam. We played leaping dolphins and lurching whales and performed underwater handstands and somersaults as the dusk dissolved into darkness and the moon rose higher in the clear, cool sky.

Finally, we wrapped ourselves in the towels Garth brought, and sat with him for a while. In his soft voice Garth described a book he'd recently read, and gently admonished me for not seeing several important movies currently in town.

As I listened, I was aware of an incredible sense of lightness in my bones, and in my heart. I found myself wishing for a freeze frame, imagining stepping out of time for a long vacation in Garth's sultry backyard paradise.

But it was nearly 8 o'clock, and I recalled an earlier scene: my husband preparing a chicken for the the oven just as I was leaving the house a few hours earlier.

I hugged Garth tight just before we left. I thanked him for inviting us to take our moonlight dip, and for the warm towels and the conversation.

"What a wonderful gift," I said.

"I don't know too many people who could get naked and enjoy themselves the way you just did," Garth said. "That's the gift."

As we headed away from Garth's house Ann pelted me with questions. Who was he? What did he do? How did I know him?

I told her that Garth had been a dancer and an actor. For a while he'd taught a great dance class on the island. I said we were old friends, and he often invited me to stop by his house, which is why I'd had the audacity to pop in, impromtu, that evening.

Oh, and for a decade, he'd owned and run a very special restaurant on Duval Street, called Savannah. Now gone.

The next evening, I was with Ann again. This time the moon was truly full, and very high in the sky when we arrived at Bobalu's for dinner. The restaurant was packed. The hostess seated us at a table with another couple. Two men. Eventually, we began to chat with them.

The food and the conversation was great. An hour passed, and then another. We learned that our new friends lived in Hong Kong and were on vacation.

Why Key West? I asked.

"We wanted to come back to Key West to eat at that wonderful restaurant called Savannah." Peter explained. "Of course when we got here, Savannah was gone."

He laughed an ironic laugh. So did I. Then I told them the story of the previous night's magic, and of Garth's graciousness, and that Garth had created Savannah.

"So you see," I said. "We've come full circle. We can say goodbye now."

And we did.

Michael Keith

*Artist Rick Worth poses in front of his painting entitled
"Wilhelmina Crossing the Seven Mile Bridge."
The mural is one of several pieces of art in public places
executed by Worth. This one's on the side of a bar, at the
corner of Olivia and Simonton.*

Center Stage

Sometimes, in the thick of the tourist season when there's no place to park, and the transient renters up the street are partying as if it were their last night on earth, the thought of leaving Key West for some quieter, less-frenzied place becomes seriously appealing.

Then summer returns. The town mellows. The poinciana trees burst into bloom. So do jacaranda. Frangipani. Yellow elder. Night-blooming jasmine perfumes the sultry air. Mangoes grow heavy, sweeten, and streak with sunset colors. Mockingbirds perch at the top of church steeples like mad angels, warbling their stolen summer songs. We walk.

Yesterday, Michael and I found ourselves on Center Street.

Outside St. Peter's Thrift Shop a kid was throwing a stick for a
three-legged dog named Kiddo. Artist Rick Worth, in a pair of
paint-splattered shorts and bathed in sweat, was in his side yard
working on a massive recreation of the Taj Mahal for La Te Da's
Survivor's Party.

It took 22 years to build India's most famous architectural
wonder. Worth has considerably less time to fashion his scaled-
down version of an ancient king's monument to eternal love,
and yet, his efforts are no less dramatic, for in his own way,
Worth is also a king, an artist of epic proportion, and a man of
love.

He is 35 years old, from Missouri, child of a broken home;
a restless student with an interest in drawing and little else.

"I had this skill, and it kept me out of trouble," he says.

Nine years ago while living on Houseboat Row, he adopted
the puppy Kiddo, and in taking on the responsibility of another
living being, grew beyond the clutch of caprice, alcohol and
other bad habits. His remaining vice is cigarettes.

"I don't want to be too pure," he says wryly. "This is a
polluted world: you don't want to become fragile."

Worth's kingdom is this Key West corner. His castle is St.
Peter's Episcopal Church, where he started out as a volunteer
mowing the lawn, and is now caretaker. Worth replaced busted-
out stained glass windows with paintings of the Black church's
forefathers. Since then he's scraped, sanded, painted and
repaired. He's done what's needed to be done.

Worth's original claim to artistic fame came from his
painted cars. You've seen them around town. Recently he
turned a Lincoln Continental into the *Titanic* and appeared in
Houston's Annual Art Car Parade. After the parade he sold it.

"I sank my *Titanic* in Texas," he muses.

Next he'll turn an old brown VW bug into a blowfish. His
paintings sell as fast as he can paint them, because they're great,
and because he prices them on a scale based upon where they

will hang.

"I understand how I price my work the way I do," he says, smiling. "No one else but me has to."

And does this king on Center Street tire of battling progress here in Paradise? Would he go elsewhere, I ask him, live someplace else?

"Oh no," he says. "Key West is growing. It's true. But I'm planning on growing with it."

"I see myself as mortar," he says, "one who fills in the gaps, saves the broken, the fading, and the wearing away so it will be here tomorrow. Someday I'll be a brick, but not now. Not yet."

Teena, at South Beach.
What's being 90 years old got to do with anything?

Unsinkable Teena Rice

L ast weekend Teena Rice held a birthday luncheon to celebrate her first 90 years on the planet. As her guests arrived at the Siam House, Teena greeted each of them with hugs and compliments. As always, she was very beautiful, in a flowered silk dress that complimented the Far Eastern decor.

On display on a table with a giant cake were two framed photos: one, dated 1907, was of pretty baby Teena. The second was of Teena today, decked out as a glittery flapper, on her way to a Fantasy Fest party.

"This is what has happened to me in 90 years," she said, holding both photos aloft.

A while ago Teena invited me to breakfast at Dennis Pharmacy. She ordered coffee and Cuban toast. So did I. Then she fished around in her big purse for 2 little jars of marmalade, ginger and key lime, that she'd made herself. We spooned the delicious jam onto our toast and sat for an hour over the bargain repast that Teena, with her stories and her joy, and her jelly, turned into a memorable feast.

Teena told me about her trip to England aboard the *QE II*. On a fluke she'd signed up for a low-cost, standby ticket. Months later, she got the call. She was sailing in a week.

"The timing wasn't good; I couldn't find anyone to go with me. But I asked myself, how many more chances will I get to sail aboard the *QE II*? Not many, right? So off I went," she said.

Assembling a wardrobe for an elegant cruise was no chore for the intrepid seamstress. All of Teena's wonderful couture is created from thrift shop finds redesigned into the gorgeous outfits that you would never, ever guess were once someone's rejects. Whatever Teena wears, she wears with flair. Being tall, and a perfect size 8 helps, too. Good genes go a long way, she says.

A London-based men's chorus was also making the crossing aboard the *QE II*. Teena was never without a dance partner or an invitation to a cocktail party.

"Fifty-five single, handsome English gentlemen," Teena says, beaming. "I felt like the Queen Mother."

After breakfast Teena showed me her new, expensive, gel-filled bicycle seat. A splurge.

"A comfortable seat is important to an old bird like me," she said, as she climbed onto her sleek conch cruiser bike and headed off to make arrangements for a trip to Albuquerque for the International Balloon Festival.

"How many more chances will I get to fly over Albuquerque in a hot air balloon?" Teena asked. "Not many, right?"

Teena was married for 40 years to a musician who was wonderful, but not ambitious. After he died, she went to Spain, where she lived well on her monthly Social Security check. On a visit back to the U.S. friends introduced her to Key West, and she found her Paradise. She's been here ever since.

At Teena's 90th birthday party, politicians, waiters, writers, gardeners, ballerinas and schoolteachers, gathered together to celebrate. I sat next to a kindergarten teacher from Reynolds School, where Teena volunteers as an aide. The children call her Nani.

"When Teena arrives I have to calm the children down," Martha Wyker said. "They surround her. They all want to hug her. I'm afraid they'll knock her over!"

One day, Martha told me, a little boy in her kindergarten class happened to look out the window just as Teena was riding by on her bicycle.

"Teacher! Teacher! Look!" he said excitedly. "Please! I want to go outside and ride my bike with Nani!"

Tom Netting

*If you knew Richard Heyman, you remember the sound
of the big, joyful laughter that erupted from him when
he threw his head back like this.*

The Mayor of Paradise

Long ago Mayor Richard Heyman and I attended a Conference of U.S. Mayors summer gathering in Charleston, South Carolina. One afternoon we traveled by bus to the Middleton Plantation, where we were served a regional dinner, and entertained by a group of gospel singers.

Richard and I skipped the cocktail hour and instead wandered away from the crowd and found our way to a gargantuan live oak tree in the nearby forest. A sign claimed the tree to be over 500 years old. It was majestic and beautifully gnarled. Richard and I sat on a bench before the tree, speechless with wonder.

Suddenly a man in a suit and tie parted some foliage and appeared on the scene. In a brash New York accent he introduced himself. He was a lobbyist, a lawyer, and upon learning that Richard was a mayor, quickly slid a business card into his hand. Then he disappeared as quickly as he had come into the picture.

Richard and I looked at each other and laughed like crazy.

Later we were loaded back onto buses. Richard grabbed a tiny bouquet of primroses out of a plastic vase from the wrecked dinner table, wrapped the stems in a paper napkin, and handed them to me. We began the long trip back to Charleston. Outside the bus windows the world was invisible, bathed in inky darkness. Inside, Richard and I shared a cramped bus seat.

I leaned against him, feeling drowsy, and as safe and warm as I ever had. At that moment I felt more joy, more well-being, than I'd ever imagined I could or would.

I have thought about that summer evening with Richard many times. And from time to time, one of us would say to the other, "Remember that big oak tree in Charleston?"

Richard Heyman's gift to the world was the great light of love he cast wherever he went. Very few people who came into his space failed to be touched by it. He was full of love, tolerance and enthusiasm.

Like his nieces and nephews from Ohio, I called Richard "Uncle Dick." Many who knew him did. One day my then 12-year-old son Mikey asked, "Exactly how are we related to Uncle Dick anyway?"

I met Richard in late summer of 1982. He was a city commissioner then, and his campaign for the upcoming mayoral race was just getting underway. One evening I was at the Pigeon House Patio bar with a group of people from the *Miami Herald*, where I was working at the time. Richard arrived with a group of politicos. He ordered a bowl of chili and sat down at a table, alone, to eat.

"Shall I keep you company while you eat your dinner?" I asked, seating myself opposite him. That was the beginning of our great friendship.

I loved Richard from the moment we met. I loved his looks, his demeanor, and his genuineness. Everything about him put me at ease, I think because he was essentially a farm boy, and I was essentially a farm girl. And although his farm had been in Ohio, and mine had been in Nova Scotia, our roots matched. On a very fundamental level, we spoke the same language.

A few days after Richard was elected mayor, he phoned me at the *Herald*, and without any ado at all, asked me if I would be his secretary. A few days later I reported to City Hall and began answering a stack of congratulatory letters sent to Mayor Heyman from well-wishers all over the world. News of his stunning victory — he'd garnered 55 percent of the votes in the primary election — had been splayed across front pages of newspapers from one end of America to the other.

Throughout Richard's first term as mayor the public's fascination with the gay mayor did not let up. The letters never stopped. Richard insisted that we answer every last one. Communication, written or oral, was of prime importance to Richard Heyman. Very quickly I learned to translate Richard's words and themes onto paper. We were a terrific team.

Politics was not my strong point; serving Richard was. I was president of his fan club, his public relations manager, and hostess. I was a confidant and best pal. And when he knew he would soon die, he asked me to arrange for a final interview and his obituary, and for a mahogany container where his ashes would be kept.

Every time I remember that Richard has left the planet, my heart breaks anew. I miss his warmth, his counsel, his phone calls, his hugs and his unconditional love. I feel orphaned. Richard's death is the most profound loss I have ever endured.

But Richard's love is also the greatest gift of my life. His strength and his courage have made me strong and courageous. His unwavering confidence in my abilities has enriched me. Through his wisdom and his humor I have learned to live well.

Richard once took his niece Marsha and some friends to London, his favorite city. Marsha was chatting with a guy in a pub, and told him of her sweet, wonderful, generous Uncle Dick.

"I wish I had an Uncle Dick," the Englishman said.

"I wish you did, too," Marsha said.

I'm with Marsha. I wish everybody had an Uncle Dick. I thank God every day that I did.

CONCH SALAD

Sanchez, on his twilight corner in Gato Village.
Mario is Florida's most famous folk artist, and a
member of the society of Those Who Knew Hemingway.

The Pope of Gato Village

Our neighbor Thea teaches history in a high school up north nine months every year. She spends her summers in Key West in the house next door to ours. From New Jersey she sends us chilling pictures of her northern home, buried in snow. She writes letters describing the long strings of dark days of her winter life, and her longing for her little house in Key West. When she arrives back in the summer, she calculates exactly how long it will be before she has to go back.

"I'm going to be here for the next 81 days," she said when she arrived in June.

It's really fun, in a vicarious way, watching Thea discover and rediscover Paradise's many charms — the food, the little lanes, the layers of history, and the people. Re-acquainting herself with the island each summer, bit by tantalizing bit, Thea spends her time here in a sustained state of enchantment.

On the walls of her Key West home Thea has hung framed Mario Sanchez posters. Mario Sanchez is her favorite Key West artist.

"There is so much to see in each picture," she says. "The details are so wonderful. Mario Sanchez reminds me of all the things I love on this island."

Thea's favorite attraction is the East Martello Museum and Gallery. She visits the place often, stopping first, of course, in the Mario Sanchez exhibit. Mario's history lessons of Key West, delivered by chunky little characters wearing brilliantly colored clothes beneath blue skies and puffy, white clouds on his carved and painted plaques of wood, speak volumes to Thea.

Yesterday, Thea arrived home from a shopping excursion, excited and happy to have completed her collection of Mario Sanchez posters.

"I think I've got them all now," she said.

"Tonight," I said, "let's walk over to where Mario hangs out and you can meet him."

In the cool of summer evenings, Mario and his brother Peruchio often sit on the corner of Catherine and Duval streets, in the heart of the neighborhood where both were born nearly 90 years ago. Mario was born in the second story of a place now called the Banana Cafe. The house where Peruchio was born is gone.

Their father was a reader in cigar factories. As the workers rolled cigars, Mr. Sanchez read to them from newspapers and novels in his famous, mellifluous voice. He was the best reader on the island, Peruchio says. The brothers can tell you where the factories were located, the names of the men who owned them and the villages that grew up around them. The village where Mario and Peruchio were born, where they sit today at sunset, was called Gato Village.

Peruchio is the talkative brother. Mario listens, and watches. His eyes are like a roving movie camera, exploring and preserving everything they see. When something in the conversation amuses Mario, he splays his strong thin fingers and claps his hands together gleefully, like a child. It seems a poignant gesture somehow, something important to remember.

So I suggested to Thea that we hike over to the visit the Sanchez brothers on their twilight corner.

"Oh I couldn't," she said earnestly. "I would be tongue-tied. It would be like meeting God. "

"Of course it's like meeting God," I said. "He's an artist."

"It's better that I admire him from afar," Thea said reluctantly. "To me he's like the Pope."

"So come and meet a Pope," I said. "The Pope of Gato Village."

Ann L. Williams

*Shine Forbes is proud of his muscles, his home on Fort Street,
and his membership in the shrinking society of
Those Who Knew Hemingway.*

In Hemingway's Corner

The story of boxer Kermit "Shine" Forbes' first encounter with Ernest Hemingway is by now a worn page in the Key West book of legends and lore. It happened 60 years ago and Shine is nearly 82 years old now, but he never gets tired of telling the story of the night at Blue Heaven when Joe Mills and Black Pye were boxing, and the referee was a big guy named Hemingway.

"I didn't know Ernest Hemingway no more than the man in the moon," Shine recalls. "I thought he was some poor bum trying to pick up a few nickels and dimes to buy another bottle."

Shine remembers how he thought the fight was getting too bloody, and how he yelled to the referee to stop it. But he wouldn't. So Shine threw a towel into the ring. Hemingway threw it back, inadvertently hitting Shine in the face. Angry, Shine jumped into the ring, and took a slug at Hemingway, who neatly side-stepped the blow and held the squalling Shine by the ears until a cop arrived.

"You're going to jail," the cop said to Shine.

"Nobody is going to jail," Hemingway said. "He's just a little excited. We're all excited. That's all."

A few hours later Shine and some pals decided that it would be the gentlemanly thing to knock on Hemingway's Whitehead Street door and apologize for Shine's bad form earlier in the evening.

Hemingway was gracious.

"I knew you'd come up here," he told them.

"I'm very sorry," Shine said.

"That's OK," Hemingway said. "We were all excited."

Then Hemingway told the young men — Shine, Iron Baby, Nassau, and Black Bob — that they were welcome to use his boxing equipment and the ring set up in his yard anytime they liked. Hemingway appreciated having the young boxers around because he loved to spar. So he created the island's first gym. And, according to Shine, it was well utilized.

Today Shine is a star, one of the last surviving members of a fast-disappearing brotherhood: those who knew Ernest Hemingway. He lives on Fort Street, in a tiny apartment plastered with hundreds of photographs and mementos from his fabulous Key West past. In Shine's yard, beneath several shading trees, he holds court. There is always room for newcomers, who are invited to pull up a chair and join the circle. And when someone takes a notion to cook, no one ever goes hungry. Throughout the day callers arrive to chat with Shine. The accidental celebrity is always willing.

The neighborhood folks who gather around Shine don't care at all about his Hemingway days. They love him for his peacemaking ways. Shine has become a very wise man, one with heart and soul. So after a couple of days of media reports about Michael Tyson's infamous snap in the Las Vegas prizefighters' ring, my husband and I decided we had a good excuse to visit Shine, and get the old boxer's take on the situation.

"Tyson was scared," Shine said slowly, after we were settled in a corner of the yard, beneath a mango tree. "He thought he could scare Holyfield with dirty looks, and then, knock him off his feet. He walked into that ring like a big bully, but he met his match. Holyfield has more upstairs than Tyson."

There are two kinds of boxers, Shine explained. There are sluggers and there are what he calls scientific types. Sluggers can beat dummies. But the scientific boxer will beat a slugger every time. That's how Ali beat Smokin' Joe. Not with slugging. With brain power.

And about Tyson's infamous bite last Saturday night?

"If it were me," Shine said thoughtfully, "my shame would take me out of the ring. For good. I would say I'm sorry. But I wouldn't ever get into the ring again."

Shine said he was concerned over what kind of message Tyson's snap into madness sent to the kids who idolize the fighter. In Shine's day, the old boxer explained, there were people like Hemingway, who gave a damn about principles, and behavior and respect. Today, there are no boxing rings where island boys might learn about fair play. It has been a longtime dream of Shine's to operate such a place. Now, of course, he's too old. Key West has turned into a resort town. And the boxing ring idea is out cold.

After more consideration Shine predicted two things. The first, that Tyson should expect to be booed if he ever does step into the ring again. And second, that Tyson, a slugger, will never beat Holyfield, a scientific boxer.

"Sometimes," Shine said at last, "It ain't about boxing at all. It's about honor."

Miami Herald

*The 7-years-dead body of Maria Elena Hoyos drew such an
audience (6,850 viewers in 3 days) that some entrepreneurial
Key Westers suggested that it be placed in a glass case and exhibited
as a tourist attraction. Her family wouldn't hear of it though, and
Maria Elena was re-buried in an unmarked grave in the city cemetery.*

Weird Science

When songwriter Ben Harrison heard the story of creepy, crawly Count Carl von Cosel, Key West's infamous necrophiliac, and Maria Elena Hoyos, the object of his ghoulish ardor, he immediately felt his songwriting senses shift into overdrive.

Harrison began performing "The Ballad of Maria Elena Hoyos" at his regular gig at the Bull and Whistle on Duval Street. Every time he did, his audience became enthralled by the weird rhapsody.

"Is that a true story?" people asked him incredulously.

"It is." Ben Harrison told them. "It really is. I promise."

Count von Cosel, who wasn't a count at all except in his own mind, was an X-ray technologist at Key West's Marine Hospital. In the spring of 1930, the beautiful, but doomed Latin beauty, Elena Hoyos, showed up at the hospital for blood tests and X-rays that revealed that she was suffering with advanced tuberculosis. Von Cosel was immediately smitten with the 22-year-old Elena, whom he recognized from a dream he'd had forty years earlier.

Von Cosel determined to save Elena's life. With his own invention. It was a bizarre contraption with electrodes that attached to the girl's wasting body. The treatments were hideously painful for Elena, but von Cosel's weird science was oddly reassuring, too. Her poor, heartbroken parents welcomed his devotion and ministrations. He kept their hopes for their daughter's survival alive.

As Elena languished in her tiny bedroom, von Cosel brought her gifts of perfume, scarves, jewelry, and exotic fruits and candies. He bought her an elaborate mahogany bed, that barely fit through the door of the family's humble home. It was in that bed that Elena finally died, on October 25, 1931.

But she did not rest in peace. One moonless night, von Cosel unearthed her nearly fleshless bones and took them to his laboratory where he attempted to preserve what remained of Elena's sultry charms with regular soaks and washes. He fought an unending battle with insects, who continually found their ways into Elena's nooks and crannies in spite of his painstaking precautions.

The madman replaced Elena's rotting flesh with oiled silk, beeswax and balsam. He replaced her eyes with glass ones.

Eventually von Cosel's eerie project was discovered. It's difficult to keep a secret in Key West — especially one as odorous as necrophilia. Seven years after he'd kidnapped Elena, she was taken from him again.

Doctors autopsied Elena's remains, and reportedly found physical evidence of von Cosel's love. He was arrested.

Elena's body was exhibited in a local funeral parlor. Nearly 7,000 people came to see her. Teachers brought their classes. Reporters came from all over the country. Von Cosel's story caught the fancy of just about everyone in America.

One day the owner of a publishing company was in the crowd at the Bull and Whistle when Ben Harrison sang/spoke the bizarre saga of von Cosel's undying love. The publisher asked Harrison if he would write a book about Maria Hoyos and Count von Cosel. He even offered to pay Harrison an advance to resurrect Key West's most twisted tale.

Harrison wrote the book, and since it appeared in local bookstores a year-and-a-half ago, it's been selling like crazy. *Undying Love* explores every mucky detail of the macabre legend and contains unbelievable quotes from von Cosel's own kooky narrative that appeared in *Scientific American Magazine.*

Next time you've got a few hours to kill (you should pardon the expression) pick up Harrison's book. Halloween Eve might be a perfect evening for this gross and engrossing read. You won't be disappointed.

The El Dorado, Havana, Cuba, 1946. Grampa is the fourth
guy from the left. The El Dorado had four orchestra pits,
and in each one, an all-girl band playing in turns.
He and his Key West friends spent many weekends in Cuba.
In those days, roundtrip airfare to Havana was $12.

Grampa's
Wild Blue Yonder

One of my extended family's favorite tales of old Key West is the one about Grampa, my former father-in-law, joining the Navy.

Mike Perez was born on Packer Street, and had never been further from home than Stock Island when he enlisted in 1943. He was 16 years old, and absurdly naive, but smart enough to alter the date on ID and trick his way into the service.

"I was looking for adventure," he shrugs, "I wanted to see the world."

At boot camp in Jacksonville, Mike was served his first taste of fresh vegetables, an experience he immediately described in a letter home.

Mama, he wrote, today I had something yellow and wonderful to eat. It's called squash, and if you ever see it in the store, you should try it. It's delicious!

Until then, his Cuban-born mother had served her family mostly beans and rice. The only vegetable he'd had was canned string beans, after which he'd been nicknamed.

"I was called 'Stringbean' or 'Jimmy Durante' because my nose was so big and the rest of me was skinny as a string bean."

The Navy changed all that. Mike loved the cuisine, and ate plenty whenever it was offered. Within a few months he'd gained 40 pounds.

"Everybody complained about the food!" Mike says. "But not me. I'd never had it so good."

Right after that first wonderful meal in boot camp, the new recruits were ordered to shower. Mike hesitated, certain that he'd somehow misunderstood the directive.

"What are you waiting for, Perez?" the chief officer asked him.

"I can't shower now," Mike balked. "I just finished eating!"

"Are you trying to make a fool of me?" the officer demanded, incredulously.

All of his young life Mike had been cautioned that certain death would follow were one to encounter water within 2 hours of eating. This applied to swimming and bathing, and even having a haircut. As a child he'd witnessed a man die of a heart attack in a barbershop chair, the result, his elders told him, of having a haircut too soon after a meal.

"So I took a shower, but I was certain it would be the last thing I ever did," Mike says. "I turned on the water, and I screamed as it hit my head. But I didn't die."

This he also reported in the letter to his mother.

The Navy enlightened him in other ways, too. He'd grown up poor, but this he did not know until he ventured into the world and began comparing growing-up stories with other sailors.

On several cross-country train transports Mike, who'd only known salt water, palm trees and summer weather, was astounded to see America's variety of topographies and climates.

He loved Oregon, and hated Maryland. When his ship anchored for a month in Baltimore, it snowed a lot and the temperature was so frigid he could not bear to go outdoors.

His ship eventually participated in the invasion of Okinawa, and Mike vividly recalls the relief and shipboard revelry when Japan surrendered in 1945, ending the war and sending his ship home.

Ultimately, he says, his great adventure taught him how much he did not know, and how much he would never know about the whole wide world.

"Now," he says, "I'm 71 years old and I don't know anything. If somebody asks my advice, I say 'You should have asked me when I was 16. Then, I knew everything.' "

Rene Rojas collection

The White Seal Bar, Miami. 1947. Henry "Basil" Gomez (far right) got his nickname because of his resemblance to the actor Basil Rathbone. Before he became the Box Man, he was very dapper and a popular young man around town. Here he is with Coast Guard buddies Rene Rojas, Mike Perez (in uniform), an unknown barmaid, and Van Gura.

The Box Man

When he died he was known in Key West as the Box Man because his only apparent possession or attachment was to a cardboard box that he carried with him wherever he went. He slept on the sidewalk, usually at the corner of White Street and Truman Avenue, wrapped in a black trench coat no matter what the weather, his head propped against his box.

That's how they found him one Tuesday night. Dead.

The Box Man appeared to be destitute, but he was not. A veteran's pension check was deposited into a bank account for him each month. From time to time he walked to the bank and withdrew cash to pay for the many cigarettes he loved to smoke. From various Cuban coffee shops on White Street he bought himself frequent Styrofoam cups of coffee. Sometimes people took pity on him and offered to buy his coffee, but he always refused their charity, assuring them he had money.

Nonetheless, he ate food forged from garbage in dumpsters behind Fausto's grocery and an apartment complex behind the Jehovah Witness Hall on White Street.

His real name was Henry Gomez. Key West friends called him Basil, after the actor Basil Rathbone. Like Rathbone, who played Sherlock Holmes in movies of the '30s, Gomez, the young man, was remarkably thin and gaunt. But he was movie-star dapper, too.

"He was one of the neatest men you have ever seen," remembers Mike Perez, a Conch who grew up with Gomez and knew him all of his life. "He was intelligent and clean. He always had a shoeshine and neat hair. He was very quiet and very nice. But there was a time bomb in him."

In 1943, during World War II, Mike Perez, Henry "Basil" Gomez, and Rene Rojas enlisted in the Navy. They went through boot camp together, but were split up after that.

After the war, the same trio joined the Coast Guard in Key West for a two-year tour of duty. Perez and Rojas were buoy watchers. Gomez was assigned to a weather station, in a lighthouse miles out at sea.

Perez recalls that Gomez stayed at the lighthouse, alone, for 90 days at a time. Then he came ashore for 30 days. Once, Gomez was somehow forgotten out at sea in his weather station, and left there for many days beyond the 90 scheduled ones.

"That's when he cracked," Perez says.

Basil Gomez recovered from his breakdown at the Veterans Hospital in Coral Gables. Key Westers Mike Perez, brothers Kiki and Rene Rojas, and Danny Boza visited him there. Eventually Gomez went to a barber school in Miami. When he came back to Key West he worked for Sam Valdez's Gate Barber Shop.

In 1976, Mike Perez moved to Houston. When he returned, six years later, he was shocked to learn that the once elegant barber, Basil Gomez, was living in the streets, filthy and unkempt.

"Like Howard Hughes or somebody like that," Perez says.

So Basil Gomez's old friends, Perez, the Rojas's, Boza and Valdez, got together and agreed to chip in and get him an apartment.

"But it was no use," Perez recalls. "Basil didn't want our help. He liked living on the streets. Nobody knows why."

When Basil Gomez died last month, his sister requested that the VA give her an American flag to bury with him, to honor his service in World War II. And she got it. Mike Perez says he saw the flag at Gomez's small funeral.

"It's important for you to tell the story of Basil Gomez," Mike Perez told me. "People should know he wasn't a bum."

*Mechi Vega, the soft-hearted proprietress of the
Cayo Hueso Kitchen, in front of her short-lived
Cuban restaurant on White Street.*

All In The Family

Every family has at least one terrific cook. In my friend Mechi's family, that cook is Mechi herself. Mechi's beans and rice are legendary, and so is her Caribbean-style lasagna. Today, I cannot go into a Cuban restaurant, or even walk by one, without thinking of Mechi. Through Mechi's family, I have been privy to the stories and tales and traditions that make this busy and evolving place in the sun ever-special, and always beautiful to me. And through Mechi and her family, I have cultivated a blind passion for Cuban cuisine.

For the last few weeks my husband Michael and I have been bemoaning the loss of our favorite Cuban restaurant, El Siboney. It's closed for a summer vacation. Tragedy! We dine at El Siboney at least once a week. We don't even try at home to cook black beans and rice, or plantains, or Italian-style liver. Nowhere but at El Siboney does the waitress call my husband Baby, and pat him reassuringly on the shoulder when the kitchen is out of his favorite white bean and collard soup.

So when Mechi phoned yesterday, I told her that we sure

were missing our regular visits to El Siboney. And Mechi told me about the time that she and her family decided to set up their own restaurant, where they figured that Mechi's magnificent skill in the kitchen would attract an army of hungry customers, and eventually make them rich.

They called the place Cayo Hueso Kitchen. It was on White Street, in the same building that today houses La Dichosa. It was a small eatery, with room to seat only 25 customers at a time. Just as the family had expected, the Cayo Hueso Kitchen was immediately packed with hungry fans of Mechi's fine cooking. They were Mechi's kids, her kids' friends, and Mechi's assorted cousins, aunts and uncles. Every day, 25 for lunch. Every night, 25 for dinner.

Mongui, Mechi's husband, stopped into the restaurant every evening after work. He would make his way through the crowded dining room, up to the register, and bang it open, expecting to find many stacks of dollars. But the cash box was always bare.

"Nobody paid!" Mechi explains. "Every seat in the place was filled by family."

Meanwhile, the town was buzzing about the apparent success of the Cayo Hueso Kitchen. Two days after they opened, Mechi's kitchen crew, her mother and her aunt, demanded a raise. The place was so packed and they were working so hard, they figured they deserved it. No raise, they said, no more clean dishes.

One day, Mechi's son Mikey remembers, a couple of tourists walked into the place. Paying customers! The employees of the Cayo Hueso Kitchen fell all over each other trying to make the bona fide diners happy, beside themselves with excitement over their first cash sale.

Another time a cash customer walked in at breakfast time. Mechi excitedly told her mother to cook up eggs, lots of eggs in every style. She did. But the customer only wanted a solitary cup of coffee.

"I cooked. I waitressed. I served the very best," Mechi says ruefully. "If I didn't have such a big family, I could have had a really fine restaurant. Instead I had a soup kitchen."

One day a very large man sat down at the counter and asked Mechi if she would extend him credit.

"I don't know why I did it," Mechi said. "But I gave him credit."

"You gave everybody credit," I reminded her.

"No," Mechi said. "There was never any discussion of credit. Just free food. But this guy asked for terms. And he seemed nice enough. So, I said yes."

The next day the man, whose name was Frankie, came again and paid his bill from the day before. He became a regular customer. One day he told Mechi that he was from Tampa, where his father had been a very fat man. Another day, Mechi and Frankie discovered that they shared the same last name. Frankie told her that his fat father from Tampa had died of a stroke. So had Mechi's. Finally it turned out that Frankie's father and Mechi's father, were the same guy.

"After that," Mechi said, "Frankie never missed a meal. And he never paid again either, because by then of course, he was part of the family."

Albert Kee at the Southernmost Point, 90 miles from Cuba.
Do the citizens of Havana hear him blowing that conch shell?
We can only hope.

Try Stealing This

Albert Kee has been taking care of business at the corner of Whitehead and South Streets since before Key West's popular tourist stop was officially dubbed "The Southernmost Point." Kee's ancestors have been selling seashells, sponges, conch and other treasures from the sea at the same spot for nearly a century.

In the late 1800's, Albert Kee's grandfather, a Chinaman, migrated to Cuba to work in a laundry. There he met his wife. The couple moved to Key West and made a meager living selling the fish they caught in the waters just beyond the point. They also gathered conch, the tough, tasty mollusk that once served as a staple of the Florida Keys diet, and also serves to name the island chain's crusty natives.

Today, beneath the same cork tree that once provided shade for Albert's grandmother as she yanked conch meat from their beautiful pink and beige shells, there is a display of straw hats atop an overturned fruit crate.

"One day," Albert remembers, "some people from the City

came along and asked us to move our stuff out of the way so they could put up a new sign."

The little sign that said "Southernmost Point in the USA" was promptly stolen. Each time the City replaced it, it was stolen. The Kees regularly reported the pilfering, but City Hall took so long to replace it each time, Albert Kee began recreating the sign himself, hand-lettering the words on slabs of driftwood.

Finally, it became clear that souvenir-crazy tourists would never be able to resist the colorful bit of island art, and in 1983 City fathers installed a massive eight-and-a-half ton cement monument, resembling a giant buoy encircled in black, red and yellow stripes, to designate the continental USA's southernmost point.

"We call this the conch challenge," says one trolley driver to his passengers, as the busy click of camera shutters fills the air. "Try taking that home."

Every 10 minutes or so a sightseeing trolley or tour train comes from one direction or the other, and Albert stops whatever he's doing and blows a mighty blast on a conch shell. The sound is somewhat like the bellow of a tuba. The delighted tourists clap and snap pictures. Albert Kee is happy to pose.

What Albert likes best, though, is talking about Key West, about his childhood memories of growing up on the point, and about how much things have changed. There are many interruptions for the friendly historian.

A middle-aged woman with an indiscernible foreign accent asks Kee to not charge her tax on a handful of postcards. He refuses with a smile.

"Taxes. Taxes. Taxes," the woman says wearily, batting the air with her hand as if to swat them away.

Albert leans closer to her and says, "Do you remember all those bridges we needed to build so that you could drive down here?"

"Yes…" she says.

"If you don't pay taxes we can't keep up the bridges," he says.

Tourists today aren't as relaxed and happy as the ones who came when he was a child and a young man, Albert says. It's like they're on furlough from prison when they get to the Southernmost Point.

"They're suspicious," Albert says. "You sense they're afraid of something."

An unsmiling man in plaid shorts and a bill hat examines Albert's $18 shell lamps and asks "do you have some smaller lamps like this, for $15?"

"Nope," Albert tells him.

"How much is this?" the man asks, holding up a brilliantly colored shell, polished to a high sheen.

"Eight dollars."

The man drops the shell back onto the table as if it's on fire.

"That's abalone, man," Albert says, as the tourist hurries away.

"Nobody trusts anybody anymore," Albert says, smiling as he waves to a couple of guys in a City of Key West utility truck.

"Hey," he yells to them, "the snook are jumping right up on shore today, man!"

Mike Perez

*A fresh generation of Conchs, growing up on the water
just like their fathers, and their father's fathers.
Danny Mira, Mikey Perez, and Arlo Haskell.*

The Great Escape

L ast Thursday night my son Mikey enthusiastically told me of his weekend plans.

"A bunch of us are sleeping out on an island tomorrow night," he said.

"Oh Mikey," I cried, as my heart clutched, "Do you really have to do that again?"

"Yes, Mom," he said. "See, it's a survival thing. We boat out and get dropped off on this deserted island before the sun goes down. No bathrooms. No water. No food. We cut open coconuts and drink the milk. We catch fish with our bare hands. If we don't catch any fish we have to kill rats, roast them on the fire, and eat them.

"It's just like *The Lord of the Flies* out there," Mikey teased, adding fuel to the bonfire of my anxiety. "You know — survival of the fittest."

It actually took me a while to realize that he was kidding. Still, I don't like the idea of a bunch of unsupervised teenagers setting up camp far from civilization, and Mikey knows that all too well.

"Please be careful," I implored "Anything could happen out there! You could get hurt! What if you need stitches? What if you have an appendicitis attack."

"Mom, you're talking nonsense," Mikey sighed.

And he was right. So I gave up, put my scary visions away, and went on without giving Mikey's camp out another thought, until bedtime Friday. Just before I turned out the light, I watched the news. The forecast for the Keys? High winds and rain.

I didn't sleep much that night, imagining Mikey and his pals on their barren island. What if they roasted marshmallows? Once at Girl Scout camp I watched as a girl was accidentally poked in the eye by her best friend's sharp marshmallow roasting stick. I remembered her being carried, kicking and screaming, to the counselor's car for the ride to the hospital.

Around 1 a.m. fat raindrops began clattering noisily onto my tin Conch house roof. The wind began to blow hard and to toss the tree boughs and plants on the deck outside my window. I imagined Mikey and his friends, huddled in flimsy sleeping bags, shivering, wet and hungry as the northern winds chilled the campsite, and a torrential rainfall doused their fire.

Poor brave Mikey! How he would suffer! And of course the campers had no choice but to await the dawn when they could jump into their boats and head for their homes. But what if pirates came along in the middle of the night and stole their boats? How would they get home then?

Just before dawn I finally fell into a thin, bad-dream laced sleep. At 8 a.m. I phoned Mikey's father on Cudjoe Key.

"They're back on shore," Mikey's father told me. "Now they're eating pancakes over at Venture Out."

Ahhh. At last I slept.

On Monday, which was Mikey's 16th birthday, he happily

told me about the camp out.

"Oh Mom," he said happily, "we watched the sun come up and it was amazing. A couple of birds flew past the sunrise. There was a sailboat silhouetted on the horizon. It was so awesome!"

"Wasn't it raining?" I asked. "Weren't you wet?"

"It wasn't raining at sunrise," Mikey said. "I think maybe it rained a little at night. But we were in our tents. We were cozy and warm."

"Did you stay up all night?" I asked anxiously.

"No," Mikey said. "We actually went to bed pretty early. By twelve."

"You know Mom," Mikey said, "there's nothing like communing with nature. There's nothing like getting away from it all.

"Maybe next time you camp out I'll go along, too, Mikey. I'd like to get away from it all."

"No. You can't come Mom," Mikey said.

"Why not?" I asked.

"Because, Mom," Mikey said impatiently. "You're a part of it all."

*Donald Lee knows our habits, our tastes, our appliances
and our ants. Here he is repairing our washing machine.
(Yes, we keep our washing machine and dryer outside on
our deck, a fact that always surprises visiting mainlanders.)*

The Power Ants of Old Town

You think you're bugged when the power goes out? Imagine how the ants feel. They apparently love electricity even more than we humans. Key West's red ants, the tiny biting variety, are willing to die for power and often do, according to our appliance repair man and newest best friend, Donald Lee.

Donald Lee knows all about our lifestyle: how often we shower, how hot we like our hot water, how frequently we do laundry, and our reverence for recorded music. Why? Because through the years, at one time or another, he has worked on all of our appliances — the water heater, the washer, the dryer, the stereo — all of their juice boxes fallen prey to our ant's suicidal fervor for electricity.

"I've been battling Key West ants for 35 years," Donald says, as he deftly removes a light switch from the wall of our century-old Conch house. He taps it lightly on a table, like one shaking for salt or pepper. Sure enough, a fine pepper of dead ants sprinkles from the switch.

"Break this open and you'll find them crammed in here so tight there's not enough room for even one more ant," Donald says knowingly.

An electrical engineer once explained to Donald his theory on why ants congregate lemming-like around the irresistible juice that will ultimately snuff them.

"He says that ants communicate on the same wavelength as household electrical power," Donald says, shaking his head incredulously. "The same frequency."

Yikes.

As Donald replaces the switch he tells us some parts of the island are more friendly to ants than others. Old Town, for example, is particularly infested.

Donald says he's as mystified by the habits of Keys ants as anybody. Sometimes he thinks ants love like the Dade County Pine in old Conch houses, or simply the aging quality of the ancient wood. Perhaps they simply prefer the excitement and the clamor of downtown living.

Some of his customers are in need of his services so often they have accused Donald of planting the varmints in their walls to make future work for himself. An absurd accusation. Donald is the fastest, and most fair-priced repairman we've known in over two decades in Paradise, and so earthy, you just know he couldn't tell a lie.

"So what can we do?" I ask Donald, as he packs up his tools.

Donald has no real solution. He says to frequently spray over-the-counter bug killer on our switches. But once it dries, he warns, its ant-killing properties dry up, too.

Is it time for another tenting and massive insect kill-off? No,

Donald says. Tenting will kill cockroaches and termites, creating a Chernobyl-like insect wasteland inside your home for years — lethal to all but red ants. The ants come back mere days later.

In our house there is a shockingly huge gecko lizard living behind a John Kiraly serigraph hung on a wall that teems regularly with long curving columns of ants, marching, marching toward their quick doom in the light switch boxes. Judging from our gecko's impressive growth, the food supply is good at the southernmost wall.

Donald urges us to keep our monster lizard happy however we can.

"He'll never go hungry," I promise.

"See you next time," Donald says, smiling radiantly, as he climbs into his truck and drives on to the next ant-ridden appliance.

The quintessential Michael Lee. He had the face of a character actor, the hands of a barroom brawler, and a heart of solid gold.

The Short Happy Life
of Michael Lee

M ike Perez once told me that Michael Lee was the only kid in the sixth grade with a car parked in front of the junior high. He parked it on side streets to hide it from his parents. Michael Lee was older than most of his classmates, having flunked a few grades along the way. Still, he wasn't old enough to have a driver's license. That didn't stop him, though. He owned a car, and when there was money for gas he enjoyed playing the big shot, picking up his buddies and driving them around Key West.

Michael Lee started drinking when he was very young, too. Drinking became a major part of his life until finally, there was no choice. He had to drink. He dried out a few times, sometimes for years, but he loved drinking and never wanted a permanent place on the wagon.

If he hadn't been an alcoholic he might have had a career in music. He really was a good singer, sensitive and intense —

sort of a Conch version of Michael Bolton.

Michael Lee genuinely liked people and people liked him back. One of his pals was Paul Linde, the actor. They met drinking at Big Daddy's Lounge in the early '70s. Michael became Paul Linde's local guide, his driver, his drinking companion, and Linde's connection to the magical and hilarious world of Key West Conchs.

In 1975, Michael Lee was hired as an extra in the movie, *Ninety-two In The Shade,* filmed locally. He hung out with actors Peter Fonda and Warren Oates. From the way he talked about it, his Conch friends were convinced that Michael Lee's Hollywood career was a sure bet. But when the movie was released only Michael's feet made it onto the big screen.

Although he drank a lot, he was not a stumbling drunk. Far from it. He never wobbled or wavered, and when the situation called for it, he was as tough and tenacious as a pit bull. Michael Lee's hands were gnarled and rough, his knuckles crisscrossed with countless scars from hundreds of barroom fights. He never backed down from anyone, and was proud of his courage.

For a while I was married to Mike Perez. Michael Lee was a regular guest in our house, and I got to know him well. He liked to smoke cigarettes, drink beer, and watch TV. When these things were within his reach, Michael Lee was content.

If you needed something picked up at the store, or somebody to help you build a new deck on the back of your house, Michael Lee was your man. You could always count on him for good company, if nothing else.

"You could trust Michael Lee with your house, your wife, your kids and your money," Mike Perez says. "He was honest."

When I was pregnant, Michael Lee was intrigued with my baby's obvious progress. As I approached my due date, Michael began to worry about the delivery.

"You know, June," he warned me too many times, "they say childbirth is the most painful thing in the world. The pain is far worse than any that a man can even imagine."

In the labor room on the night my son was born, I clung to Mike Perez and shivered in pain. Mike solemnly remarked, "Looks like Michael Lee was right, huh?" And we roared with laughter.

Just before Michael Lee died of oral cancer a few days ago, he selected a song to be played at his funeral. His friends predicted it would be his old favorite, the one he loved to sing anytime a local band would let him step up to the microphone and perform. It was "Knights In White Satin," by the Moody Blues.

"It was the one song he knew all the words to," Mike Perez says.

But the song Michael Lee chose for us to play at his funeral was singer Taylor Dane's powerful version of "I'll Always Love You."

And he did.

Handsome, funny, smart Mike Perez, my favorite Conch.
Our marriage didn't last but our partnership in parenting
was a big success. To wit, our son, Mikey.

His Key West

For a long time I was in the cozy habit of a daily telephone chat with my old friend Mike Perez. Every afternoon I'd call him. Or he'd call me. Ostensibly our conversations were about our son, who is 17 years old now, the result of our short, long ago marriage.

But Mike and I always found lots more than our boy to talk about. We talked about what was going on in his family. In mine. The weather. Controversies. Jokes. Deaths. Marriages. How much Key West has changed.

Mike had the keys to my house. I to his. When he was away we'd feed his dog. When we were away he checked on our place.

Through the years Mike has fixed plenty of things at our house — silly things that most people can handle without professional help. As he installs a curtain rod, or tightens a door handle he mutters and shakes his head.

"Intellectuals," he says.

And yet, I've sometimes repaid his favors with music.

During the course of our relationship he's developed a taste for Beethoven, particularly piano and violin sonatas.

A few months ago my husband and I drove to Miami with our son and Mike. Mike, who's always been one of those guys who has trouble sitting still, drove our car while we sat in the back seat. All the way to Miami he entertained us with funny stories of growing up in Key West.

When he was a little boy, Mike said, the DDT trucks regularly rolled through neighborhoods, releasing dense clouds of mosquito poison. The children would gather together and follow the slow-moving truck, gleefully dancing in the weird smoke of DDT fumes. If he and his cousins misbehaved, their grandmother Norma would warn, "You kids better be good or you won't be allowed to play in the DDT."

And that, Mike said, was an unbearable thought. The DDT truck was a thrilling high point in their lives.

When I told him I was worried about whether or not our son would be able to get into the college of his choice with a barely B average, and unremarkable SAT scores, Mike told me not to worry.

"I went to school with a lot of guys a lot dumber than our kid," Mike assured me. "And they graduated from Key West High and went away to college and got degrees. They're big shots today."

Six months ago, one of those educated big shots Mike grew up with offered him a job developing land in Central Florida. On New Year's Day, Mike told me he'd decided to leave Key West. A month ago he finally did.

"He's a Conch," his mother said to me. "He can't stay away from Key West for long. He'll be back."

But I'm not so sure. His departure felt very real to me. And in many ways, it made a lot of sense. His Key West, the island he introduced to me 20 years ago, with its unpainted buildings grown silver in the sun, all-night parties on Smathers Beach, and sweet, dumb innocence, is gone. The son we raised is grown and ready to fly.

A few days after his father left, my son pulled out an old photo album of his baby and early childhood days. Many of the photos feature Mike and me. Young. Proud. Happy.

"Does it make you sad to look at these old pictures of you and my dad?" my son asked.

I thought about my answer for a long time.

"Not at all," I told him. "Having a baby was a lot of fun."

"I guess this is it," Mike Perez said, mocking drama on the day he left Key West. "I guess it's finally over between us."

"Oh no," I said, dramatizing back at him. "It's not over between us. And it never will be!"

"I guess I can't shake her!" he shrugged, as he shook my husband's hand goodbye.

CELEBRATIONS

My tall, Cuban ex, Mike Perez: The Unknown Champ

The Unknown Champ

A sure way to attract the attention of everyone in a crowd, I discovered on a recent Florida vacation, is to be introduced as one who lives in Key West. Key West is a hot topic up in Amerika.

"What's that big street party you have down there?" a guy at a Saturday night party in Gainesville asked.

"Fantasy Fest," I answered.

"Isn't that coming up soon? You're going to miss the big party!" he warned, rolling glazed eyes.

"Ah, well," I sighed. "You see one Fantasy Fest parade, you've seen 'em all."

That's not true, of course. It's just that at that moment I wasn't up to a long-winded diatribe on the differences between what Fantasy Fest really is, and what the rest of the world thinks it is.

The very first Fantasy Fest parade, 18 years ago, featured a local hippie named Sister posing as a figurehead on a boat that rolled down the street on wheels. Sister was painted from tip to stern in bluish-silver paint that glowed in the dark. She looked like an angel. Sister held her head held high, as she led off the premier Fantasy Fest parade. Her lovely breasts, like happy beacons, pointed the way down Duval Street. The whole scene was so beautiful it brought tears to your eyes.

The next year, or that year (the years tend to blur), the Key West Business Guild decked out a small army of beautiful, young men with kohled eyes in gold loincloths, upper-arm bracelets, and head pieces. In the middle of that stunning army, that seemed to stretch for an entire block, King Tut was carried aloft on an elegant throne.

One year, when an act called the Unknown Comic was the big deal on TV, I made a red satin robe for my tall, Cuban husband. Across the back of it, in white block letters, "The Unknown Champ." He wore with this his boxing gloves and boxing boots. Over his head was a brown paper bag with eye holes and several band-aids.

It was an incredibly cool costume. As we walked down the middle of Duval before the parade, we were greeted by the flashing and clicking of many cameras.

But there was a creepy response to the costume, too. Big guys kept coming up to the champ and challenging him to fight. Pretty soon it wasn't funny anymore and my husband accused me of setting him up. I'm no longer married to him, and that clever costume is probably among the reasons why.

Last weekend I visited a former Key West pal in Cape Canaveral. Sabrina took me to a clothing-optional beach where she was scheduled to rendezvous with her newest flame, an all-American looking Kennedy Space Center engineer named Will.

I was naked and shivering, hugging my knees to my chest to ward off the late afternoon breeze, when my old girlfriend introduced me to her new boyfriend. Whether I was shivering from the temperature or the audacity of what I was doing I could not tell.

Sabrina introduced me to Will, adding, "June's from Key West."

"I've been to Key West twice, for Fantasy Fest," Will said, as he quickly slipped off his jeans and shirt and took his place on our blanket.

The first time he'd gone, Will said, he hadn't had a costume. The next year, he did. He wore a seedy trench coat and tie. Anytime anyone looked his way, he would pull open the coat, flick a switch, and a huge penis, created of foam rubber and pantyhose by his space center secretary, would boing into view. This, he said, was some of the best fun he'd ever had.

"Oh my God!," I said, suddenly scrambling for a towel. "You're one of those guys?"

"Fantasy Fest is a big sex party, right?" Will asked, bewilderment suddenly flashing on his apple pie face.

"I mean that's certainly how it looks to an outsider," he said. "Like a big sex party."

Jamie Hunt

Margot drinks a toast to the dimming dusk of the waning summer with a cup of mango tea.

Garden Variety Lunatics

Season begins roughly around this time each year, just before Fantasy Fest. You feel it in the cool evening air. You hear it in the throbbing of the downtown drums on Goombay Festival Night. There is a ripe harvest moon. It's the beginning of the silly season. Suddenly there are so many things to do. Goodbye summer doldrums. Hello autumn zest!

In my neighborhood there is a tea party every Thursday night between 6 and 8 p.m. In the past few weeks, during the indecisive and hazy last weeks of summer, there has been some confusion over exactly when tea time actually is. More than a few of us, it seems, encounter difficulty in negotiating the vapory area between the dimming dusk of the waning summer, and the burnished dawn of the tropical autumn. This is a treacherous time for lunatics.

But at the autumn tea I felt myself easing through the changing of the seasons with grace, clarity, and many cups of mango tea.

We knew we'd found the tea party when we saw a sign on

the 300 block of Petronia Street that said "Invite Someone Dangerous to Tea." A man with a Mohawk haircut, dyed pink, bright pink, and green and brighter green directed us to a path that trails past the bakery and into the garden. The outdoor theater/garden/tea room is called Behind Heaven, and it is covered with many banana plants.

Upon the stage the play *St. Joan* was recently performed. Poetry is read here, too.

The guy with the multi-colored Mohawk reappeared wearing a triple-tiered black negligee and strapped high heels. He snapped photographs with a serious-looking camera. In New York he would be called a club kid. I recognized him as the waiter who served my pecan pancakes last Sunday at the Blue Heaven.

A handsome black construction worker named Michael modeled a shirt created of African mud cloth. The designer is Marschia Thoms, whose father, the artist Walter Thoms, lived in Bahama Village for many years. Marschia sits at our table, in a stunning jacket, also made of mud cloth, and tells us how she became interested in designing clothes. The family TV set broke down when she was 12. Her father, tired of his children fighting over what to watch, refused to replace it. So Marschia took up sewing, knitting and cooking.

In the late 1960s, she enrolled at the Fashion Institute of Technology in New York City. Hey! I went to school there, too! Excitedly we compared notes. Turns out we were both big fans of FIT's phenomenal dining room, where thousands of would-be fashion writers, illustrators, designers and merchandisers gathered to eat the memorable cuisine.

Then, it was time to sample the crumpets. Jamie, our host, confessed that he had forgotten to clot the cream the night before, so we had to make do with peach honey.

At the table next to ours sat a very regal drag queen in a black skirt and white lace shirt. Her hair, steel gray. Her breasts, large and pointy. Her hips, ram-rod straight. I think I recognized her as a guy who runs an antique store downtown. She examined the table of offerings; egg salad sandwiches, scones, chocolate candies, and key lime tarts topped with meringue.

"I only want this," she said at last, her black eyelashes fluttering as she nibbled a slice of cantaloupe.

"Marschia," I said. "We really haven't wandered so far from that FIT dining room."

I visited Jay Border, the guest psychic. The fat full moon was rising behind him as he invited me to shuffle the Tarot cards for a reading.

"Any questions you'd like answered?" Jay asked.

"Just don't give me any bad news," I said. "And oh, yeah...I'm a lunatic. Did you see the full moon last night?"

"It's actually not quite full yet," Jay answered, rolling his eyes.

Jay expertly flipped the Tarot cards, and told me the meaning of each one. The cards said I had a secret to reveal, and that a man I trust will soon sabotage me! The cards also said I am lately releasing a bunch of kundalini energy and that I should be feeling it often. Jay explained that it's like electricity racing up and down my spine. Hot. Cold. Hot again. It's my serpent power, and it's a good thing, he said.

Whoa! And I thought I was having hot flashes!

Sabrina Maxwell

*An old photo of me in the summer of 1976, wearing my
Jimmy Carter for President T-shirt, and taking a break on
the Appalachian Trail. Twenty years later, I had the
opportunity to show it to President Carter. He loved it so much,
he autographed it for me.*

Spirit of '76

After only one week as a museum help temporary, I qualified as a staff member at Truman Little White House, and as such was invited to be at the museum with the other employees to meet President and Mrs. Jimmy Carter as they arrived for a dinner party on New Year's Eve.

At first I couldn't decide whether or not I wanted to stand outside the Little White House just after dusk to greet the Carters. For one thing I didn't feel like a true staff member, and for another, I was afraid of being seized with celebrity stage fright.

But whenever I mentioned to anyone that I might meet President and Mrs. Carter, they were intrigued. Everyone I know calls Jimmy Carter their favorite president. And so I decided that I owed it to my friends, and my future grandchildren, to go.

In an old scrapbook I found a picture of myself taken in the summer of 1976, right before I moved to Key West. In it I am wearing a Jimmy Carter for President T-shirt, taking a break from a hike on the Appalachian Trail. It was the summer of the Tall Ships in New York, and the U.S. Bicentennial. It was a time of high spirits and great hope. Everywhere you went, everybody was crazy for Jimmy Carter.

In a raucous Key West bar, a few months later, I watched the amazing election returns on television as America made the sunny man from Plains, Georgia its 39th president.

I had my little picture blown up to page size, and carried a pen with me to the Little White House on New Years Eve. Having a mission, I figured, would save me from being nervous, and it did. But it didn't save me from being thoroughly awestruck when I met President Jimmy Carter and the gentle Rosalynn.

The Carters moved with lightening speed through the short line of Little White House employees. The President approached each of us with his hand extended, ready for shaking, a benevolent smile on his face. He's the kind of man who makes you feel warm and special, all in an instant. And he exudes the unmistakable glow of greatness.

"It's a great pleasure to meet you, President Carter," I said brightly.

"We're honored to have you here, Mrs. Carter," I said to Rosalynn. "Welcome."

And then, they were gone. That's when I remembered my picture and my mission. I found a handsome teenager in the Carter party and showed my picture to him. The kid, who exhibited a junior version of the President's magnanimity, was Chip Carter.

"My grandfather would love to see this," Chip said.

So I busted out of formation, and ran up ahead to the other end of the line. Meanwhile, Chip approached the President and said, "Grandpa, a lady here has a neat picture to show you."

The President turned around and looked as I held up my picture.

"It's me, in 1976, on the Appalachian Trail," I blurted quickly. "See! I'm wearing a campaign shirt that says 'Jimmy Carter for President.' Do you see your face here?"

"I love this picture," he said, beaming.

"Would you like to sign it?" I asked.

"I'd be honored," he said, and without hesitation, using his right leg as an impromptu desk top, quickly signed my photo.

And then, it really was over.

I can't remember what the Carters wore, or how their faces looked. What remains in my mind is the memory of a sensation of belovedness, the Carter's embodiment of hope — and that unmistakable glow of greatness.

Kenley Jones

*Michael Keith, father of the bride, Susan, and her sisters
Meredith and Laura. Everyone is wearing the same smile,
but only the girls are wearing high heels.*

Adventures In Gender Bending

Just before he left Greenville, South Carolina, my husband Michael played the part of Jerry/Daphne, a cross-dressing bass player in the musical *Sugar*. Michael's first order of business, upon landing the most challenging role of his career in community theater, was to find a comfortable pair of high-heeled pumps.

At Belk's Department Store, Michael carefully tried several pairs of size 9 wide, before deciding upon black, two-inch heels, close enough to the ground to keep him from wobbling, high enough to lift him into the unmistakable realm of feminine illusion.

"The sales ladies could barely stifle their giggles," he recalled.

"Did you tell them you were buying the shoes to wear in a play?" I asked.

"No," Michael grinned. "My motto back then was 'never

complain. Never explain.' "

Today, no doubt, there are still people in Greenville who titter and whoop when they recall the businessman, Michael Keith, who donned a pair of pantyhose to do *Sugar* at the Greenville Little Theater and, at the end of the show's brilliant run, ran off to live at the end of the road, Key West, forever after.

In fact, Michael's adventures in gender-bending ended when the final curtain came down on *Sugar.* I have not yet had the pleasure of seeing my husband as Daphne, but I am no stranger to drag. I know a man in woman's clothing when I see one. And I love it.

That's why I'm going to be at the head of the line at 7 p.m. Monday when La Te Da opens the flood gates to the 20th Annual Survivors Party, themed this year "The City of Eros."

On the long list of the events scheduled for the biggest and best Survivors Party ever are performances by drag queens like DDT and Trish Blonchette, divas like Vicki Rousch and Suzy Michaels, musicians like Bobby Nesbitt, Billy Nine Fingers, and Gordon Ross, and, a special, you-won't-want-to-miss-this, number by Ricky Regretto and Goo Goo Lenore.

The first Survivors Party was held at the Monster Bar on Memorial Day of 1975. Then, as now, tourism wound way down by the end of May. To boost morale during bleak financial times by raising funds for the even less fortunate, a guy with the only-in-Key West name of "Ma" came up with the idea for the survivors party. (Born in the middle of a brood of 11, John Evans babysat so often his little brothers and sisters began calling him "Ma" and it stuck.)

Today, Ma Evans, a tireless and brilliant party maker, fundraiser, and ultimate diva of drag, is still producing the Survivors Party in addition to a thousand other community events he helps organize. One October, Ma was elected King of Fantasy Fest with $ ballots totaling $26,000 for AIDS Help. Survivors parties, which began 22 years ago, raise $20,000 or more in one glittering night of community spirit.

Survivor's Parties are always slated for Memorial Day. They feature fantastic food, cash bars, spectacular entertainment and a very campy awards ceremony performed on a stage constructed right across Duval Street. There are collector-quality T-shirts. There is dancing and schmoozing on Duval Street, which is closed to traffic in the vicinity of La Te Da from 7 p.m. until midnight. If not this year, some year, you gotta be there, or you'll be pegged square.

Oh, and if you ever see me with a very cute guy named Daphne, eat your heart out. He's mine.

Michael Keith

*Mike Perez, Senior, "Grampa", knows the secret of true
happiness: a lot of appreciation for anything at all.
Here he beams upon receiving soap on a rope for Christmas.*

Stars On Their Ankles

Mike Perez, Sr. grew up in Key West during the Great Depression, and though his family, like most on the island at that time was very poor, he says he did not know it.

"Sometimes I wondered why my parents didn't eat with the kids," he remembers. "They would say 'go ahead and eat. We'll eat later.' They did that because there wasn't always enough food for everybody. So, they would go without."

Every week Mike would pull a wagon, fashioned by his father out of an apple crate, four wheels and a piece of rope, down Division Street, which is Truman Avenue today, over to the corner of Whitehead and Southard streets. That's where the WPA (Works Projects Administration) center was located, where the Green Parrot Bar is now.

"We would get our rations there — flour, sugar, and so forth," Mike recalls. "I waited on line, put the stuff in the wagon, and then pulled it home again."

When Mike was 9 years old he made a routine trip to the

WPA to pick up food and received a wonderful surprise: a little red jacket, and black sneakers, with little stars on the ankles. He could hardly sleep that night in anticipation of the next morning when he would show off his finery at the Truman Elementary School.

"I felt so sharp in that jacket, and so proud wearing shoes without holes in the bottoms," he says. "I walked to school feeling really good. Then I got there, and saw that every kid was wearing the same thing — a little red jacket and black sneakers with stars on the ankles."

In those days, a really good Christmas was when his father found a beat-up bicycle frame in the city dump, straightened it out, put a couple of new tires and a fresh coat of paint on it.

But there was no such thing as a bad Christmas back then, Mike says. A boy wasn't lucky enough to get a bike every year, but there was always a toy for each child. Boys received little cars or trains carved in wood. For the girls there were dolls fashioned from scraps of cloth by their mothers, or tiny tea sets, created out of recycled tin cans and paint.

"Whatever we got, it was fabulous!" Mike remembers. "We were so happy to get anything at all."

In spite of their poverty, there was always plenty to eat on Christmas Day: rice and beans, and roast pork. The family's many relatives came for dinner. They ate buffet style, sitting throughout the tiny Conch house, anywhere they could find seats.

Then everyone went to Bayview Park. In the afternoon a siren screamed toward the park, bells clanged, and a fire truck arrived to deliver Santa Claus. He carried a huge sack of gifts, and sat in the middle of the bandstand. Kids stood in line and waited patiently to receive their gifts, little toys and rare goodies to eat like nuts, tangerines and oranges, all provided by the WPA.

"Later the adults would dance to various bands from

around town," Mike says. "There was something going on all day. Nobody left. Nobody was there alone. Families partied together. Then, by 9 p.m., everybody was home again."

Tomorrow Mike Perez, who is 71 years old now, will spend Christmas Day with his son's family. He will watch his grandson open an endless pile of gifts, more gifts than he could have ever imagined when he was a boy of the same age.

"I enjoy seeing him so happy with all those things he gets at Christmas time. I get a kick out of it," Mike says. "But you know, I feel kind of sorry for him, too. I can't help thinking that kids today are in for some big disappointments down the road. It takes so many gifts to make them happy."

Susan with Key West friends Leslie, and her sister, Lisa.
Leslie once taught Susan an important lesson about the
Christmas spirit. Ten years later, Susan named her daughter after her.

Bah Humbug House

Breaking with tradition by remaining in South Florida for Christmas all these 22 years since arriving in Paradise, has been, for me, akin to wrestling a powerful addiction. Christmas at my New England family's house was a time of savage stress and furtive attempts at Currier and Ives yuletime perfection that never quite jelled. The queasy memory of that yuletime dysfunction, mixed with sweet memories of the aroma of baking turkey and simmering cranberries, provokes a potent stew of conflict.

Because of my mixed emotions, coupled with the lack of snow and frigid temperatures, I've never been wholeheartedly engaged in, or been sincerely infused by, the spirit of Christmas in the tropics.

I haven't set up my artificial Christmas tree since my son became a teenager. My excuse is that there's no room for it in my tiny house, when in fact, the lack of space has been in my heart. Houses on either side of ours are bedecked in lights, red ribbons and garlands of evergreen at Christmas time, while our own cottage stands unadorned. We laughingly call it the Bah Humbug house.

My husband Michael has a wonderful Key West Christmas story. Eleven years ago, his beloved father became very ill just days before Christmas. Michael and his daughter Susan were sharing a house then. They were very sad. And broke, too. So they ignored Christmas and hoped and prayed for Michael's father's recovery instead. When Susan's wise and compassionate friend, Leslie Artique, learned of the situation, she arrived at the house with a live spruce tree and boxes of decorations.

"You've never needed the Christmas spirit as much as you do right now," Leslie said.

They decorated the beautiful tree, and really were cheered by it. Michael's dad died, and Susan and Michael flew home for the funeral. It was understandably the saddest time of Michael's life, and certainly the saddest Christmas.

But there is the mitigating memory of Leslie's Christmas tree, and her kindness. The story of Leslie's Christmas tree is a happy footnote to that sad event, and today an important part of family lore. Michael tells the story of Leslie's gift whenever the subject of Leslie, or her restaurant, the Old Road Cafe, come up in conversation. Susan, who lives in Birmingham today, named her only daughter after Leslie.

Still, I have remained indifferent to Christmas icons like trees, wreaths and Santa hats. But all of that changed last Saturday night, when I stood on the corner of Truman and Duval, and watched the gloriously funky and profoundly joyous Key West Christmas parade.

Michael and I hadn't planned on watching the parade Saturday. The air had turned chilly and we'd been working hard all day, vacuuming, airing blankets, scrubbing floors, preparing our house for holiday visits from our grown kids. But as the parade began to pass our block, we heard it. Moreover, we felt it. The excitement and the joy of it seemed to seep through the walls of the Bah Humbug house, like the aroma of roasting turkey and simmering cranberries. And so we went.

As we stood among our neighbors, watching the bright eyes of happy toddlers held aloft by their parents, children scrambling for candy tossed from floats, and the jubilant arrival of Santa Claus himself, I felt young, and hopeful and happy and wildly in love with my town and its amazingly diverse citizenry.

Today, right after our son Mikey arrives home for Christmas vacation, we'll put up that old artificial tree, and remember all the good things that it stands for.

*Dennis Bitner, one of the first of many friends I loved and
lost to AIDS. Dennis owned and operated the now-defunct
Club Key West Baths.*

The End of the Rainbow

On Thursday, International AIDS Day, I stood in a large crowd and listened as a long list of names of local people who'd died of AIDS was read aloud on the Monroe County Courthouse lawn.

We were gathered around the sign that says "The End The Rainbow." I felt the names plunk through the surface of my consciousness like pebbles, tossed one by one, onto the placid surface of a still pond, launching a ripple of soft, sweet memories.

Larry Hill, the actor, was a waiter at the Claire Restaurant. He was also a patient at dePoo Hospital where, during the mid-'80s, I worked in public relations.

On the day Larry learned he had AIDS, we sat together in the hospital lobby and cried. Larry had never told his parents he was gay. (Apparently they hadn't seen his performance in *The Boys in the Band* at the Red Barn Theatre.) He dreaded that he had to tell them not only that, but also the sad news of his illness. As it turned out, they were supportive and loving up till the end, which for Larry, came very quickly.

Tom Puroff worked in public relations at Florida Keys Community Hospital. With much in common, spiritually as well as professionally, we fell into an easy friendship. As hospital workers, we watched in horror as the AIDS drama began to unfold. Sometimes on Sundays we sat by Tom's pool, drinking coffee, reading the papers, and sharing our thoughts. Tom was very frightened that he might develop AIDS.

"I saw this guy with AIDS interviewed on the news the other night," Tom once told me worriedly. "I'm sure I knew him."

Tom was tall and tan, with bright, blue-green eyes, a quick smile and a marvelous wit. He was a good person, who cared a lot about others. Watching him sprawled in his pool chair, glowing in the sun, I remember thinking he was too good, and much too young, to die. But Tom's worries were not unfounded. He eventually died of AIDS, too.

George Lee, the artist, was my dear, wonderful neighbor. Intelligent, moody and devastatingly handsome, George was a trusted friend with a memorable comic sense. George managed Millie's, a sundry shop on Front Street that caters to cruiseship passengers. One day I asked George which sundry cruise passengers bought most often when they came into his shop.

Laxatives, he quickly answered. George had become an expert on over-the-counter constipation remedies. My husband Michael and I laughed hysterically as he recounted absurd conversations with his desperate, cruise-cuisine-sick customers. The impromptu routine was as funny as any stand-up comedian's, and we begged to hear it often.

Danny Fleming worked on Richard Heyman's mayoral campaign in 1987. Danny and my husband grew up in the same town: Greenville, South Carolina. They even looked a little bit alike — blond, blue-eyed, wiry and chic, they could have been brothers.

My favorite memory of Danny is of him and Michael

tallying votes on the election night party when Richard Heyman became Key West's mayor for the second time. Danny and Michael wore tight blue jeans and plaid shirts. Their eyes glittered with excitement as they watched for the precinct totals reported on TV. They huddled together, clicking away madly at their calculators, tallying the winning scores on that great night of victory.

Thursday, somehow Richard Heyman's name was not on the list of those read aloud, though he also died of AIDS. As I listened to "Amazing Grace," Richard's favorite hymn being played on the bagpipes at the end of the ceremony, I imagined what he might say about that.

"Did you call to make sure my name was on the list?" he would ask, the way he did when he was the mayor and I was his administrative assistant.

"Uh, no," I would answer. "I just assumed it would be."

"Oh, I see," he would say, smiling radiantly. Richard would never say "Oh, I see. You messed up." Even when you really did mess up. His magnanimity is what I remember best about him. About all of them.

Michael Keith

Neither my brother Donald nor I ever knew our father,
who is buried in the church cemetery behind us in this photo
taken in Malagash, Nova Scotia. Until a few years ago,
we didn't know each other, either.

Indian Giver

My mother told me my father's name the spring I graduated from high school, 18 years old and badly bruised from a lifetime of being ignored by the man I'd believed to be my father.

I had a stepfather, who I probably should have appreciated much more than I did. But I wanted my real father, the one who left when I was very small.

"Take good care of your mother, Angel," he'd whispered as he hugged me goodbye. Then, the man who'd terrorized my mother and me with drunken rages as often as he charmed us with sweet singing and funny stories, was gone. He returned to Canada, while we stayed in New York.

Christmases and birthdays passed with no word from my real dad. I grew up. When I needed money for college, my mother suggested that I look up my real father, who'd reportedly sobered up, and done well in business.

"I don't want anything from him," I replied angrily. "I don't even believe he is my father. A real father wouldn't forget his own flesh and blood."

Mom didn't sass me for my outburst, or warn me, like she usually did, that bitterness was a deadly poison. Instead she blushed.

"You're right," Mom said at last. "He isn't your real father. Do you think you're ready to know the truth?"

"Yes," I said, barely breathing, a lifetime of longing suddenly crushing my heart. "Who is my real father?"

"Your father was a wild Indian," she said.

Instantly, I conjured the image of a television-movie Indian replete with headdress, war paint, loincloth, and tomahawk. Then, my mother, just 16, innocent as Little Red Riding Hood, walking through the Canadian woods. The wild Indian jumping out from behind the tree. Nine months later, she was still a little girl! — I was born.

"A wild Indian?" I said.

"Well, not really an Indian," Mom smiled. "I just mean a really wild guy."

"Where is he now?" I asked.

"He's dead," she said.

So I found my father. And a heartbeat later, I lost him again.

When my mother became pregnant, my father Donald did not marry her. When she was 6 months pregnant, he married someone else to whom he'd long been engaged. Shamed and frightened, she married the Jekyll and Hyde monster who took us to New York and left us there.

Three years later, Donald was killed in a mine in Quebec. He was 27 years old, and left behind two babies, a pregnant wife …and me, the daughter he never acknowledged.

My mother learned of his death in a letter. Every bone in his body was broken, the writer said. When she read the words, my mother told me, she felt as if her soul was falling and falling, for a very long time, like my father's lean young body just before he died.

Eventually, I found my father's people. My grandparents gave me a picture of him. They took me to his grave. I know my father's three sons, and they know me, far better than any of us ever knew him. Sometimes my brothers and I get together in the Nova Scotia town where we were all born, and imagine what he must have been like. We know so little about our dead, wild Indian father. He loved to sing. He loved to dance. He was a peacemaker. He was a great guy and everybody loved him. So how could he have turned his back on my mother and me?

I think of Donald on Father's Day. I do not hate him for the betrayal I will never understand. Sometimes I forgive him. Sometimes I can't. Some days the pain of being a fatherless child is like being on fire. Some days I know it doesn't matter, that I am whole in spite of what he kept from me.

If he were here today, he'd provide a plausible explanation. That's a bastard's crazy hope. My father would make everything right...Wouldn't he? But if he could make it right now, why couldn't he then? In all these years of trying to understand my father's heart, my own heart has become a monster of ambivalence, a battleground of compassion versus contempt.

The mystery is my father's gift, and his curse. It is his legacy.

Capt. Tony collection

Jimmy Buffett on stage, beneath the sign that says:
"Everybody is a star at Captain Tony's."
But not everybody is a drunk.

Last Call at Captain Tony's

Eleven years ago last night, I had my last drink. It was Spring Break, 1985 — one of the first Spring Breaks, when Key West was still reeling at the number of kids jamming onto the island. A Channel 7 news team had come from Miami to document the phenomenon. A girlfriend at the assignment desk at Channel 7 had given them my number. They called just after I got home from happy hour at Claire's Bar, broke — but very happy.

Would I like to spend the evening showing them around? You bet I would. Dinner at the Full Moon Saloon, preceded by several cocktails, was on somebody's Channel 7 expense account, and so were the drinks that followed.

There is wonderful status in guiding a film crew, complete with a camera plastered with the Channel 7 logo, through the bars of Key West. Everywhere we went, we were welcomed with good cheer and an endless flow of free beer.

Last stop was Captain Tony's Saloon, where we received our best reception of all from the king of revelry himself: Captain Tony. Among the famous captain's many charms was his knack for making certain no one's glass ever reached empty.

The next morning came much too soon, but I made it to work on time. I always did. I prided myself on my ability to pull myself together after a night of carousing. I was strong. Invincible — except for a niggling ache in my side. I had made an appointment to see a doctor, and it fell on the day after Captain Tony bought me my last drink.

I was very frightened that day, as I sat on the examining table in my tissue paper gown, while a relentless hangover headache pounded in my temples. A glass of wine would turn all that misery around. It always did. But lunch was two hours away.

"How much do you drink?" was a question on a list the doctor asked.

"What do you mean?" I said, the way people do when they're stalling for time or hoping for a miracle.

"How many drinks did you have yesterday, for example," he asked.

"Fourteen," I said, too miserable to lie. "Two at lunch. Four at happy hour. Two at dinner. And six beers downtown."

"Of course, yesterday was an unusually long day," I added hopefully.

Then, the miracle. At that precise instant, denial stopped working for me. In a flash, I saw a terrifying truth. I had become what I most hated and feared as a child — the thing I'd long promised myself I would never be. An alcoholic.

"Oh, no, you're not an alcoholic," my mother insisted. "You just like to drink. We all like to drink in this family."

"Alcoholics are bums lying in the gutter," a good friend said. "You're certainly not like that."

"You only drink wine or beer," another friend said.

"Alcoholics drink the hard stuff."

It is amazing how eager so many people were to ease me off the hook, help me avoid the pain of facing my problem. It is also amazing how many more people were willing to help when I needed help most. Learning to live sober is a hard trip, but when the going gets rough, you're never alone. It is a very busy highway.

Today marks the 11th anniversary of my last hangover. But anniversaries don't mean a lot to me anymore. Remission from the disease of alcoholism doesn't happen a decade at a time. Or a year at a time. It happens a day at a time. And that, I've learned, I can handle.

TIES THAT BIND

Roger Henley

*Tropical Gothic. Michael and me playing Martha Stewart
and preparing to garden on a friend's farm in
Cumberland County, Nova Scotia.*

It's A Good Thing

My husband loves Martha Stewart. Every night, at 11 p.m., he watches her television show. We discovered Martha by accident one restless night a few weeks ago. And now we never miss her.

"Who is this woman?" Michael said on that first night, suddenly sitting straight up in bed in rapt attention as Martha assembled a trellis in the back yard of her New England country house.

He thinks Martha is a model woman. He likes her clothes. He likes her hair. He likes her ideas. He's mad for her kitchen and her strawberry pots and her baked apples that make a whole house smell like a Currier and Ives Christmas.

His favorite Martha Stewart program so far was the making preserves show. Michael is the kind of guy who gets lost in the jams and jellies aisle at the grocery store. The more expensive and exotic the blend, the more likely it is to spend the next two years of its life in our refrigerator. But no more. From now on, we're making our own.

"Think of the possibilities," Michael says. "Key limes. Mango. Guava."

And as a result of my husband's new fascination with Martha Stewart we no longer buy fresh picked herbs. We grow them ourselves on our back deck. Like Martha.

"She's very earthy. Even when her hands are covered in dirt, Martha is able to maintain her elan," Michael says. "Not too many women can do that."

This weekend we're painting flower pots. Martha and Michael are tired of terra cotta.

Michael believes that watching something creative like the *Martha Stewart Show*, just before going to sleep, is good for the imagination.

"From every show you get four great ideas," Michael says. "Then, while you're sleeping you process the information. It's a good thing."

Sometimes Michael falls asleep midway through Martha's show. The next morning, of course, he begs me to tell him what he missed.

"Martha was real earthy last night," I told him the other day. "She made sandwiches out of ingredients from her garden — baby lettuce, basil leaves, and cherry tomatoes. Then she slaughtered this cute pig she'd raised in a pen next to the compost heap. After she butchered Pork Chop — that was the little pig's name — she made smoked ham for the sandwiches."

"Wow," Michael said, turning pale. "I'm glad I missed that."

"I had nightmares," I said. "So much for processing good ideas."

Recently, I came across Martha Stewart's biography on the Internet. Martha is from New Jersey, made a killing in the stock market, and owns several country homes. She and Michael are the same age. Martha was married, but her husband left her to run off with a woman 30 years younger.

These facts I dutifully reported to Michael, who seemed

saddened by the news of Mr. Stewart's betrayal.

"She won't have what Martha has," Michael said ruefully.

"Right," I said. "She's 30 years younger."

"You think it's easy to talk to a 25-year-old woman?" Michael said.

"I don't think talk is necessarily what he's looking for," I said.

Then, at 10:55 p.m., I switched off the television and turned out the lights.

"Hey!" Michael yelled. "What are you doing?"

"No Martha Stewart tonight, honey," I said. "We need to talk."

Sabrina Maxwell

In John Kiraly's garden, on Thanksgiving Day.
Twins John and Joe Knox, Mike Perez (the tall one),
me (in barefeet) and our son Mikey, leaning on
the Chuck Dodson sculpture.

The Wisdom of Solomon

L ike many kids in the Keys, my only child has been raised in two households — his father's and mine. It's been this way since he was 3 years old.

After the divorce, Mikey's dad and I agreed to a dual custody arrangement. But we battled terribly about who should get Mikey, and when. Finally, we divided a calendar in half and shared him. My share of Mikey's life was Tuesdays, Thursdays and alternate weekends. The other half of his life, he spent with his dad. It worked something like a sit-com plot in which two good friends buy a car together and ruin their friendship as each try to get their fair share out of the deal.

It was a lousy system. Inevitably, something Mikey wanted would end up at the other house where he wasn't — toys, sneakers, bike. In each of Mikey's homes there were different bedrooms and different bedtime stories. Different values. Philosophies. Cultures. Mikey's heart, like his life, seemed torn not very neatly in two.

Eventually, Mikey's dad remarried and bought a house 20 miles up the road. Weary of his disjointed lifestyle, enamored of up-the-Keys style living, Mikey, then nine years old, asked to move to Cudjoe Key with his dad. Agreeing to the move was excruciating for me. A psychologist friend counseled that Mikey needed to live one life. In one home. The move would be a good one for him, she said. Besides, the distance of 20 miles was not so difficult to negotiate. As it turns out, she was right.

Shortly after Mikey was established in his new life up the Keys, something very scary happened. I was in Miami, dining with a friend and her family, when my friend's mother asked about my son. I explained that he'd chosen to live at his father's house.

"You gave him up?" she gasped, dropping her fork, her eyes wide with horror.

People don't usually express their misgivings so boldly, but it's there. There is a powerful prejudice against a mother who allows her children to live with their father after the divorce. Of course, when the father agrees to allow the kids to live with their mother no one thinks twice.

The bottom line was what worked best for Mikey, I told myself during many moments of uncertainty. Was he healthy? Was he happy? Was he well cared for? Yes to all of those things. He loved his big bedroom, in his big house on a canal. He had a boat. A dog. A rope swing. A bicycle and safe, wide streets to ride it on.

On holidays and on birthdays, we began having extended family celebrations. All of Mikey's parents have shown up for his ball games, his concerts, parent nights at his schools. Now that he is about to leave the Keys and fly into the big world beyond this little one, I'm acutely aware of how much we've missed by not having a day-to-day relationship. But I'm also recognizing how much we've gained.

When parenting time is limited the way mine has been, you

parent very concisely. Because your opportunities to teach are occasional, you pick and choose your lessons carefully. And when parenting time is limited, you love lavishly, without restraint, and without resentment. My son and I have not had time to develop the inevitable contempt bred by familiarity.

My friend Andrea believes children should be raised communally. Even Hillary Clinton says it takes a village. Which is why the celebration of Mother's Day sometimes takes me back to that dinner table in Miami, when I was accused of "giving up" my son.

I'm a lot tougher today. I'm a very confident mom. Still, it's not easy to go against the tide, to break with tradition. Fortunately, here in Paradise, the road less traveled is a much more comfortable ride.

*Joey Arena, on his final birthday, with his sweet sister
and my oldest friend, Sandy.*

Red Ribbon Days

I'm just home from a ten-day stay in New York. I grew up there, in a tiny, postcard-pretty village, just 50 miles, or an hour train ride, from New York City. I still have two brothers and several good friends back in New York, and when I visit there I try to see as many of them as I possibly can.

In visiting them I meet many other people, and everyone, it seems, has a question or a comment for a girl from Key West.

"How come you're so white? Why don't you have a tan?"

"You don't have seasons there, do you? I couldn't stand that."

"Is it anything like that television show? No? I didn't think so."

"Are the streets full of Cuban refugees?"

"My brother/friend/neighbor/girlfriend/cousin/oil man/manicurist moved there. Nobody has heard from him/her since."

"I want to go there. I want to go there bad."

Usually, I get a kick out of the questions and the

comments. Usually, I respond to each and every one. But on this visit I did not promote Key West with my usual high spirits. These days I'm not particularly passionate about anything at all.

I went to New York for a much-needed change of scenery. I thought that travel to the places and the people most familiar to me might help my dark mood. I'm in a hazy, half-alive state of mourning, where nothing seems to feel, taste, sound, smell, or look nearly so wonderful as it once did before my best friend died five weeks ago.

I thought that New York with its many distractions, its fantastic autumn weather and brilliant natural colors, would feel somehow soothing. And it did. But I found myself feeling most comfortable with people who were suffering recent losses, too.

My brother Rocky's lover, Kathy, lost her daughter to cystic fibrosis two years ago. I stayed at their house, a warm cottage deep in the woods. Nights, my brother built huge fires and we three gazed wordlessly into them until we fell asleep. Days, while Rocky was at work, Kathy and I talked a lot about her bright little girl, Jenine, who endured a 20-year long lifetime of illness, but never lost her sense of wonder or humor.

Sandy, the girl with whom I shared my first cigarette in a junior high girls' room, my first season in Ft. Lauderdale, and some of the best fun imaginable, recently lost her brother to AIDS.

We made arrangements to meet at Sandy's apartment, and to go to lunch from there. Sandy's mother was there, too, and the minute I walked in we three sat down and cried together for long minutes.

Later, as Sandy and I were leaving, her mother pinned a red AIDS awareness ribbon on the lapel of my jacket.

I was wearing the same jacket, still with that ribbon, on the flight home last night.

"What does that red ribbon mean?" A guy in the next seat asked.

"Where are you from?" I asked him incredulously. "What do you do?"

"I'm a physician," he answered blithely. "I live in Baltimore. What does that ribbon mean?"

"It means I've lost someone I love to AIDS." I answered.

"Oh gee, what happened?" he asked. "Did your hairdresser die?"

"No, my best friend," I said. "On September 16th."

In another seat a mother was nursing her baby. The physician watched her silently for a few seconds and then turned to me and asked: "If you could be reborn, would you choose to be a man or a woman?"

"A woman," I answered, crossing my arms over my chest, turning to the window, and closing my eyes.

"Why?" he asked.

"Because women are intelligent and sensitive," I said. "And they make much better conversation than men."

RICHARD A. HEYMAN
MAYOR~ EMERITUS
KEY WEST, FLORIDA
1935 - 1994

*"Your looks are laughable, unphotographable,
Yet you're my favorite work of art.*
*Thank you for 22 years of light,
love and laughter.
With love always, John*

*John Kiraly created this quilt panel of Richard Heyman
for the AIDS Quilt. The cow jumping over the moon is
evocative of Richard's childhood on a farm in Ohio.
The butterfly on his finger refers to his gentleness.
The stairs lead to a door to the other side of the universe.
The lyrics are from their favorite song, "My Funny Valentine."
That's Gracie Sparks, Richard's good friend and
longtime housekeeper, standing next to the panel.*

How Do You Spell Tears?

There are a number of island people who will say, come Monday, "Hey! The AIDS Quilt is gone already? It wasn't here long! I was going to see it! Now I've missed it."

So don't miss it. It's not like a movie. It's not like you can catch it when it comes out on video. You've got to go now. Although it will hurt and stun you, it will also calm and soothe you and open a new place in your heart.

Thursday, the first day of the exhibit, my husband Michael and I spent an afternoon as Quilts in Paradise volunteers. Our station was the front door where we greeted people as they arrived. Tourists, I noticed, entered quickly, striding into the room to begin viewing the famous quilt. Locals entered with much more trepidation.

"I'm dreading this," one man said. Then he smiled and pointed to a huge white hanky stuffed into the back pocket of his jeans. He shrugged. "But I have to do it."

"I'm worried about how I'm going to handle this," a woman said, scanning the huge display from the door and hesitantly moving into the room.

Michael and I watched people arrive, view one or two panels, and then break down. Most people cave in right there, at the beginning, when the enormity of the thing hits with a force that almost knocks them off their feet. Then they recover, push their shoulders back, and move ahead to see 400 more panels, representing 400 more people who were once so alive, so loved, and are now so dead.

Sometimes people said to us, as they were leaving, "my brother is over there. See? Right there." Sometimes they came out in shock, having just learned that someone they knew had passed on and become a part of the quilt since the last time they saw them.

Michael and I viewed the quilt for the first time in the morning. Four busloads of students were there, too. That's when I cried the most, the first time through, although throughout the day the crying never really stops. It's like a funeral, where most people are negotiating a queasy balance between laughter and tears. There are boxes of tissues located at the corners of each quilt section.

The school kids were remarkable. Quiet. Somber. Many of them broke away from groups to take in the panels alone, at their own speed.

A volunteer watched a group of junior high kids viewing a panel, when one of them said to the others, "Hey, I was born that year, too!" and then, "This girl was only 4 years old when she died." He turned to the nearest adult, who happened to be a volunteer, and said in a voice full of amazement, "I didn't think little kids could die of AIDS. I thought you had to be 19 or 20 to get AIDS."

Later in the afternoon the crowds thinned, and there were

times when the only people in the room were we volunteers, dressed in white — white shirts, pants and shoes. A guy wearing black jeans and a black T-shirt came to the door and in a low voice asked Michael, "do you have to wear white to come in here?"

After a few hours at the door, when numbness had settled in my heart and my bones, I gazed into the room, squinted, and blurred the walls and floors swathed in a thousand hues of colors into a giant smudge. I felt I was seeing the dying embers of a blazing fire, the scene of a massive tragedy that had killed hundreds of men, women and children.

Then I saw the man in the black jeans and the black shirt. Deep in concentration, he was writing in a comment book at the exit. Suddenly he looked up and asked a volunteer, "How do you spell tears?"

Eileen Hammill

*Our great friend John Kiraly (whose work graces the cover
of this book) and Mikey drawing together in 1988.
Mikey was just 9 years old then, still our baby, not
yet vulnerable to spring's bewitching powers.*

What I Forgot To Say

It was a beautiful, balmy spring evening, the last Saturday night of Spring Break. Sixteen-year-old Mikey and a friend heard about a party in a nearby Cudjoe Key neighborhood. Just after dark, they rode their bicycles to the party being hosted by a couple of 14-year-old babysitters. When they arrived there were three other boys there. Then another showed up with a bottle of vodka and a hookah pipe. Later, another kid showed up with a bag of marijuana. And the party was under way.

The kids cranked up the stereo and danced in the Florida room. The babysitters passed out tumblers of vodka mixed with Juicy Juice.

Mikey had never been drunk before. He'd never been able to cultivate a taste for alcohol. Beer tasted awful. And the slug of whiskey he'd swallowed on a dare months earlier had gagged him memorably. But vodka in Juicy Juice was another story. It went down easy. It almost tasted good.

Empowered by the vodka, the kids arranged themselves in

a semi-circle around a coffee table to smoke marijuana from the hookah pipe. Even before his turn came, Mikey felt very good, high on the camaraderie, the liquor and the hormones, thick as springtime sap, boiling in his veins. He toked deep on the hookah.

"Is that good stuff?" a strange and decidedly unfriendly voice suddenly boomed from somewhere behind him.

Mikey's stomach clutched violently as uniformed deputies entered the room, confiscated the pipe and the pot, and directed the kids to phone their parents. The deputies had been summoned by neighbors complaining about the loud music.

As parents began to arrive, Mikey began to vomit. Since he had been the one with the pipe in his mouth when the deputy walked through the unlocked back door, he was charged with possession of marijuana. The others were charged with possession of drug paraphernalia.

As he listened to the deputy and watched his only son cradle his head in his folded arms, Mikey's father felt as if he was watching his high-flying dreams for his boy being shot out of the sky like hapless birds.

Mikey had been an almost perfect son. A happy baby. A sweet and funny little boy. A loving kid, full of hugs and kisses and I-love-you's. A boy who seemed to have enough self-esteem to hold his own when the peer pressure steamed into high gear. A boy you could trust to do the right thing, or so his father had thought. Till now.

Now Mikey seemed a stranger, drunk and sick and shamed. The boy, who was just over six three now — could barely walk. He certainly couldn't ride his bike.

"How did you plan to get home tonight, son?" his father asked him, as he helped fold Mikey's floppy limbs into the back seat of a car for the short ride home.

"I didn't expect this to happen," Mikey answered miserably.

It was just midnight when I received the phone call here in

Key West from my ex-husband, telling me about Mikey drinking and smoking pot and being charged with possession of marijuana.

It was very difficult for me to imagine my sunny kid drunk. Or stoned. Helplessly, I recalled countless conversations I'd had with Mikey about alcohol. Pot. LSD. Cocaine and crack. About AIDS. About dishonesty. Indifference. Prejudice. I thought I'd covered every conceivable danger that Mikey might encounter outside the soft cocoon of his family's unconditional love.

But finally I remembered what I'd forgotten to tell my son. I'd forgotten to warn him about spring. How, when you are 16 years old, spring can make you feel reckless, invincible and lonely all at the same time. And how sometimes, that terrible mess of conflicting emotions can make you do some really stupid things.

I knew, because I'd done them, too.

*Daughter of Hope. Baby Claire 8 weeks after a Miami
tornado provoked her early and much heralded arrival.
A happy, red-headed girl with blue eyes, and the cool,
clean energy of a spring whirlwind.*

Tornado Baby

Tuesday morning my old friend Patty, who lives in Miami, went into labor two weeks before she was scheduled to give birth to her first child. I heard the news when I arrived at work.

"Your girlfriend's water broke at 4:30 a.m.," Jennifer, the receptionist, said excitedly. "She called at 8:30 to tell you. Call her right now! Let us know how she's doing!"

I was charmed by Jennifer's enthusiasm. She's never met Patty. The two women live in different cities, and even different worlds. But Jennifer is a mother, too, and on this day, they were sisters.

The day felt momentous and important. I wanted to remember every detail of it, but my mind was so jittery I could barely remember my name. I calmed myself with frequent reality checks. The facts were these: Patty is a superb athlete, a practitioner of yoga, a vegetarian. And the baby, who would be named Claire, had been declared perfect in every way amniocentesis could measure. Most calming of all, I was not the one giving birth.

"We're very busy here this morning," a nurse told me, when I finally got through on the phone to the maternity floor.

"The tornado started everybody's labors," Patty said when I finally got through to her. "I sound pretty chipper, don't I?"

She did. Then "Ouch. Ouch! OUCH!!"

"Breathe, Patty!" I said.

I called Jennifer, and then my husband, to report on Patty's progress. I read the horoscope for one born on May 13. I checked the headlines in the *Key West Citizen* and then tucked the papers away to deliver to Patty for Claire's baby book.

Although it's been 18 years since I'd last been in Patty's shoes — or should I say stirrups — I clearly recalled my own labor and delivery, before the days of ultrasound and amniocentesis, and back when I believed a baby could save a marriage.

A favorite activity for my son's birthday is to recount the story of his birth. It was a windy day, I say. There was a lone pine tree visible from my labor room. The labor was short. Mikey did not cry, but rather cooed when he entered this world. Seconds later he looked long and hard into my eyes, and then into his father's.

"It felt as if the hand of God reached down and squeezed you right out of me," I tell him.

Some day, I will tell Claire about the day she was born, and of how I waited here in Key West for her safe arrival, so nervous I could barely push the buttons on the phone to make reservations to fly to Miami and meet her.

Just before I went to bed, I called the hospital one more time.

"Push, Honey," I heard the nurse who answered the phone say. Then "Hello?"

It took a few minutes to find her, but finally I was connected to Patty in the recovery room. She was weary, but very, very happy. Claire had not cried, either, when she was born. And like Mikey, she'd stared hard into her parents' eyes. She was peaceful, sleepy, and beautiful, Patty said.

Patty told me about the hospital lady who came for information for Claire's birth certificate. She was confused that although Patty was not married, Claire's dad Kevin was very much there.

"So you'll put your name here where it says 'father'?" the lady asked tentatively.

"Yes, of course," Kevin said proudly. "I am Claire's father."

They met at massage therapy school. He's gay. Patty's straight. They're both single. They've become best friends, in a warm and sharing relationship more tender that many lovers ever realize. Patty wanted a baby. So, after much deliberation and careful planning, they made one. Claire is created of love and passion deeper than flesh; of life's longing for itself.

Maybe someday Patty will show her daughter the valentine Kevin gave her shortly after they met, and a year before anyone had even thought of the possibility of Baby Claire. It said: *Roses are Red. Violets are blue. If I were straight, I'd marry you.*

It was the most romantic valentine she'd ever received, Patty said.

Mimi McDonald

Did you know children's book author Shel Silverstein wrote
"On The Cover of the Rolling Stone" and "A Boy Named Sue"?
Here he is at Captain Tony's Saloon surrounded by Key West friends.
(Left to right) Baby Courtney, Linda, and Chuck Krumel,
Ritchie Krumel, Shel, Gary McDonald, Toni Tarracino,
Captain Tony Tarracino, and Susan Nadler.

This Rock Won't Roll

My brother Rocky is a man of few words. Nonetheless, he phones me regularly. Now that he is a grown adult, aged 30-something with a job and a phone bill of his own, he no longer calls me collect from phone booths during the furtive predawn hours. Nowadays, he calls way before bedtime.

Yesterday, Rocky called to say he's considering a move to the Florida Keys. The woman with whom he has shared his life for the past 15 years, the woman whose name is emblazoned across his heart in a glorious red, purple and blue tattoo, has grown silent and untouchable.

"What do you think is the problem?" I asked.

"Eh, I don't know," my baby brother answered.

We do not have in-depth conversations. We never have. Time with Rocky is spent listening to music, or watching television, or driving through the beautiful New England back roads where we grew up.

Last fall I visited Rocky. To demonstrate the stunning

capabilities of his new stereo he played the song "On The Cover Of The Rolling Stone."

"I bought this whole CD just to get this one song," he said.

"Shel Silverstein wrote this song," I said excitedly, suddenly spotting an inroad to possible conversation. "He lives in Key West!"

"Oh yeah," Rocky said.

We were eating takeout pizza and I, ever hungry for possible topics of conversation with my elusive brother, commented on how good it tasted.

"I don't know why," Rocky said, "but there is no pizza anywhere as good as what you get here. Outside of Connecticut, New York and New Jersey I've never had a good pizza. I don't know what it is. The humidity? Something in the water? I wonder about that."

I was struck dumb. It was the longest speech I had ever heard him make.

One of Rocky's hobbies is ice fishing. He likes photography, too. Last year he sent me a self-portrait of himself posing on the ice, dressed in a thermal jumpsuit. In it he looks like a big, brown polar bear, patient and content, the only living thing on a long, lonely expanse of white snow and ice.

Two winters ago he sent me pictures of his new house, a sweet little cottage in the middle of the woods, with a chimney and a stone wall surrounding it. Since Rocky bought his own house I always ask him during our telephone conversations how things are going with it.

"We had to put on a new roof," he told me during a call a month ago.

"Wow, that sounds like a big job," I said.

"Eh, it was all right," he answered.

Lately, Rocky has been calling more frequently than usual to discuss his moving plans. I am thrilled with the prospect of having my baby brother within hugging distance again.

"Maybe we'll get a bigger house and we can all live together," I suggested.

"I think I'll live up the Keys a ways," Rocky said apologetically. "Maybe I'll buy a little tackle shop and live upstairs."

"And what about your house in New York? Will you sell it?" I asked.

"Eh, maybe," he replied.

"You can put your Harley in the back of your Blazer and drive down," I suggested.

"If I still have the Blazer by then," Rocky said.

"By when?" I asked.

"About two years," Rocky said.

"Two years!" I exclaimed. "Rocky, I thought you were coming now."

"No. Not now," he said. "Some day. But I'm coming."

So is Eli. So is Godot.

My friend, the prodigy: Eugenie, in 1966. We were only 16.
With her music, she gave me tantalizing glimpses of the world
beyond the little country town where I lived and she weekended.
Back then, she was the most dazzling, sophisticated girl I knew.

Roll Over Beethoven

R ecently my good buddy Carolyn told me she'd read that rats listening to Mozart found their way through a maze faster than those listening to something else. What else? Snoop Doggie Dog? Wynonna Judd? John Philip Sousa?

"What happens to rats listening to Schubert?" I asked.

"The article only mentioned Mozart," Carolyn said.

I like listening to the "Trout Quintet" when I write, envisioning myself a happy fish, swimming easily through the difficult waters of composition, buoyed by moody Schubert's rippling phrases.

Still, I considered Carolyn's Mozart news. The job of writing is not, after all, very different from being a hungry rodent fighting its way through a confounding maze. Could Mozart help me find my way? It was worth a try. I plugged Mozart's "Requiem" into my player...and completed the first 33 pages of a novel I have long dreamed of writing.

Just kidding.

A while ago I discovered that I could quite easily locate

long lost friends via my computer and the World Wide Web. One of these was a pianist named Eugenie. When we were kids, Genie's family had a weekend home near mine in upstate New York. During the week she stayed in New York City and went to school there. Weekends she came to the country where her somewhat Bohemian parents maintained another home. I was often invited to her culturally lavish house to hang out. She was dazzling, small and beautiful; the most sophisticated girl I knew.

Genie practiced on a baby grand piano, improbably jammed into a tiny study off the living room. She played for hours every day. Even on weekends. I loved watching her tiny hands blurring over the keys. It was impossible to read (books were my refuge then) while Genie played. I could only listen in awe. She played a lot of Chopin that season of our friendship, and the experience began my lifelong devotion to Chopin's dreamy music.

We fooled around a lot, too. Genie played a full-blown version of "The Star Spangled Banner" while I bellowed the words in baseball stadium soprano. I played the flute. She taught me songs like "Smile" and "Satin Doll" and the theme from *The Umbrellas of Cherbourg*. We worked a Handel flute and piano sonata to perfection. I still have the music, with Genie's pencil markings vaguely evident on it, to this day.

When Genie got her driver's license, we spent Sunday afternoons driving about the countryside in her parents' Volkswagen, smoking cigarettes and talking about boys.

She told me about her boyfriend Tad, who put hot jazz on the turntable when they necked.

"He knows it drives me crazy," she said, smiling mysteriously.

We grew up and lost touch.

Through the years I imagined my old friend Eugenie as a great diva, playing concerts on every continent. One day I found that her college listed its alumnae on the Internet. I found her address. I could have written. But I was too excited. I phoned. Genie answered.

She teaches music at an Ivy League college. She's married to Tad. They have two grown daughters. She did not remember me.

"We played the theme from the *Umbrellas of Cherbourg*," I said. "You cried when you told me about the movie."

"I cried?" she said, perplexed.

"We were sixteen," I said. "You dyed my hair red and I sang the "Star Spangled Banner" like Kate Smith."

"I dyed a lot of girls' hair red in those days," she laughed.

"You drove a VW and you made me love Chopin," I said weakly.

"Chopin?" she said, as if she'd never heard of him. "But my favorite composer has always been Mozart."

A big yes to romance. Our wedding day in 1988.
Mayor Richard Heyman married us in his back yard,
in front of a lush gardenia bush that flourishes still.

Blood, Sweat and Ten Years

Twelve years ago I watched my 85-year-old grandmother fighting for her life in a hospital intensive care unit. She was hemorrhaging. Six units of blood were pumped into her before surgeons were finally able to find and repair a hole in her stomach. Later, I learned the blood that kept my grandmother alive through that terrible day had been collected by the American Red Cross.

Gramma recovered completely, and I became a dedicated, card-carrying blood donor, with a wallet-sized Red Cross ID. I encouraged everyone I knew to do the same.

I met Michael Keith around that same time. I was recovering from a broken heart, and after many months of seeing him, I wasn't yet sure if I was ready to try love again, even with someone as dear as Michael. So, I bided my time, not saying yes to romance; but not saying no, either.

One day I invited Michael to come with me to donate blood. I was late to arrive to our blood drive date. I found that Michael had started without me. He was lying on a white-sheeted table, wearing a blue chambray shirt that matched his eyes, his fist squeezing the gripper they give you to keep your blood pumping smoothly out of your arm. He smiled when he saw me, like he had a hundred times before. I smiled back.

Suddenly I was jolted by a hard shock to my heart, a blow as piercing as Cupid's arrow. Zing! I was in love! My knees buckled. My heart pounded. My view blurred with tears. I nearly fainted right there in the doorway, before giving the first drop of blood.

A month later we moved in together. A year later, we married. This week, we celebrate our tenth wedding anniversary.

In those early years of our romance, donating blood stayed an important ritual, a way of giving back, a feel-good exercise, and great justification for a lavish and fortifying meal out.

One day we showed up to donate blood and I was turned down. Not enough iron, they said. The next time we tried Michael's blood pressure disqualified him. So who needs that mean bee sting stab in the soft crook of your arm? By then we'd given gallons. Enough already. It was somebody else's turn.

Michael and I lost the habit of donating blood, and, through the years, many others, too, like celebrating small things with big cheer, and treating each other as tenderly as if we'd just lost a pint of blood.

Recently, we learned that the American Red Cross was having a blood drive, and collecting blood samples for the National Bone Marrow Donor Program. We wanted to be registered for that. So we went, signed on, and qualified to give blood, too. Nowadays I've enough iron, and Michael's blood pressure is down. We're blood donors again.

We'd forgotten that giving blood can actually be a lot of

fun. The Red Cross workers who fill out the forms and poke your arm are the most genuine, personable and charming people the world. I guess they have to be, right? And they're damned good at making the bloodletting just about painless.

Giving a couple pints of blood is a weird way to celebrate a tenth wedding anniversary, but it made sense to us. Marriage, after all, is a bloody enterprise. You feel good to have done it, entitled to big cheer over small things, and justified in the enjoyment of an occasional lavish and fortifying meal out.

Rocky Mazza

Self-portrait in a doorway. My brother Rocky, surrounded by
his favorite things: fishing rods, electric bass, oil painting of
himself by a onetime girlfriend, and a cigar box of family pictures.
This house, where Rocky lived for several years, was the smallest
occupied dwelling in Westchester County, New York.

The Windchill Factor

I was watching the weather channel when my brother Rocky phoned from up north. The scene on my TV screen was pretty bleak. The reporter's breath condensed in great foggy clouds around her face each time she spoke, as she described the massive snowstorm battering New York City. Behind her, snow was falling like crazy. Pedestrians were slipping and sliding. Taxis were colliding. Schools were closing. Airports were shutting down.

"Wow! The weather's pretty terrible up there, huh?" I said to Rocky, who lives 50 miles north of the city.

"Nah," he said, with tough guy nonchalance. "It's not bad."

"It looks like a blizzard on TV," I said.

"Yeah, I guess it is," Rocky said. "Hey, it's Christmas-bonus time. I got a bunch of envelopes here I haven't even opened yet."

Rocky is a garbage man, which makes him, employment-wise, the most successful of my siblings. On top of his great salary, each year he collects a small fortune in Christmas tips from his satisfied customers. And each year he calls me on the phone to brag about it.

"Why don't you open up a couple of those envelopes and buy yourself plane ticket and come down for Christmas," I suggested.

"I don't need to open these envelopes to come to Key West," he chuckled.

Last summer when his romance crashed, he decided to move to the Keys, a move he's been seriously considering since the first time he came here years ago. For a time it looked as if he really meant to come. He sold his house. He announced to his boss that he was leaving Westchester and the garbage business. He subscribed to Keys newspapers and began hunting for property.

"I gave my boss a year's notice," Rocky told me.

"You did?" I asked incredulously.

"Yeah. I did," Rocky said. "And he gave me a raise."

Just before he called the other day, I'd mailed a Christmas card to him. In it I asked him why we hadn't heard much from him lately. But I think I know the answer. The last time we talked he said he'd spent Thanksgiving with Kathy, his on-again, off-again girlfriend of 13 years.

"They'll be back together by Christmas," my husband Michael predicted.

"I went hunting last weekend," Rocky told me.

"Did you shoot anything?" I asked.

"Nah. I never shoot anything," he said. "I just like to walk around in the woods. I stayed at Kathy's."

Uh-oh, I thought. But I didn't scold my baby brother for being a fool for love. I'm no one to talk.

"So is it real cold there?" I asked, steering the conversation away from the news I did not want to hear.

"Yeah, and I've been thinking," Rocky said. "It's 27 degrees up here today. With the windchill factor it's like 10 degrees. And you know what I'm wearing? A T-shirt. And L.L. Bean pants. Green, 'cause it's Christmas."

"If that's what you wear when it's 27 degrees in New York," I said, "what are you going to wear when it's 92 degrees in Key West?"

"See, that's what I'm saying," Rocky said. "I'll have to go naked. I'll have to live on an island and kill my own food."

"You're going to live on lizards and birds?" I asked.

"No. I'm thinking I'll go to one of those monkey islands. Eat monkey meat," he said.

"They're putting them in cages now," I said.

"Then they'll be easier to shoot," he said.

We made a couple of monkey jokes, and then Rocky said, "The house next door to Kathy's is for sale. It's beautiful, on the crest of this woody hill. I can get a real good deal on it."

"What about monkey island?" I asked.

"Well that's just it," he said. "You know I could never kill anything."

otton

*John Jay High School drama club nerds Ellen Reich and
Stuart Ross, performing a scene from* The Fantastiks.
*Ellen's brother Bobby later became President Clinton's
Labor Secretary. Stuart wrote* Forever Plaid, *a big theater hit.*

Forever Stuart

I n the final scene of the film *Pee Wee's Big Adventure*, Pee Wee tells his friends that he doesn't need to pay particular attention to his life story reenacted on the big movie screen. Why not?

"Because," he says, "I lived it." Then he prances off into the night.

That's how I felt when I saw the play *Forever Plaid*, written by my old high school buddy, Stuart Ross.

In high school, Stuart Ross was a nerd. Glasses. Braces. A tad chunky. He was in the honors class, an insular group of overachievers with big IQs and proportionately small social skills.

I was a member of that group of social retards, too, though my scholastic track was pretty hopelessly derailed the first time I heard Jim Morrison sing "Break On Through to the Other Side."

Meanwhile, Stuart's interests remained wildly out of sync with the generational madness of the '60s. In or out of school he wore khaki pants, button-down shirts and sensible shoes. He played the trombone in the school band. While the rest of us were saving up for the next Rolling Stones album, Stuart was carefully mapping out his career in serious showbiz.

He was a member of the drama and the audio-visual clubs. In a variety show he sang "Pardon Me Miss, But I've Never Been Kissed by a Real Live Girl," with such conviction and charm, you'd think he'd been born backstage at the thousandth performance of *The Music Man*.

In spite of his nerdy ways, I liked Stuart. But it was through show tunes that we became real friends. He and his girlfriend, Ellen, introduced me one day to the music from *The Fantastiks*. I was so smitten, I rushed out after school to buy my own copy of the album.

A small clique of *Fantastiks* lovers grew at our high school. And the next year our school play was, guess what? *The Fantastiks*, with Stuart and Ellen in the lead roles.

I did not see Stuart again for many years. Then, around 1983, he showed up in Key West. He'd just graduated from EST training. I'd just become divorced. We met for cocktails at the Monster Bar. He moved into my house that afternoon, and spent the next few weeks typing furiously at my kitchen table, and conversing frequently with his agent in New York. Then, he disappeared from my view once again.

In 1990, I got a phone call from Stuart.

"June, I've got a hit!" he said. And he did. His show *Forever Plaid* was packing them in off-Broadway, and Stuart was suddenly a star. Writer. Director. Choreographer. An overnight success in, as he put it, "only 15 years, 7 weeks and 3 days!"

"I'm making lots of money," he said in an infrequent phone call several years later, "but I don't really have time to spend it. Crazy, huh?"

When *Forever Plaid* came to Miami's Coconut Grove Playhouse, Stuart invited me to opening night. What a thrill! At the cast party, he introduced me to his friends, saying "In high school June and I were the dumb kids in the smart group."

Later, as we drove along Miami Beach in his rented Lincoln Continental, Stuart told me how proud he was of me, and how impressed he was with my happy life in Key West. My husband. My son. My little Conch house.

"But I'm still a loser," I said, in a fit of self-pity over my lack of artistic success. "I still feel like the dumbest kid in the smart group."

"You'll always feel that," Stuart laughed. "But don't you see, June? That's what *Forever Plaid* is about. It's about you and me and other people like us. The kids in the audio-visual club. The ones who auditioned for every school play. The four-part harmony groups who wanted just once to sing on a stage and get paid for it. People like us, who never learned to stop dreaming."

Eden House

That's Goldie Hawn riding shotgun, but it could be me, right Shep?
P.S. I'm still at the same phone number…

Hooray for Hollywood

A Hollywood producer named Shep Morgan called our house last week to say he might be interested in turning my book, *Postcards From Paradise*, into a film project. Would we be interested in discussing the matter further, Shep asked my husband Michael.

"Sure," Michael said. "Why not?"

By the time I got home from work, a 10-page fax had arrived from Pentacom Productions, and my son and husband had decided upon who they wanted to portray them in the film version. Shep's Hollywood resume was introduced by a friendly cover letter, full of praise and gusto.

"I think there are boundless possibilities in *Postcards From Paradise* that range from a feature film to — I'm serious — a sitcom that could leave Dave Barry's in the dust," Shep wrote.

June Keith is not making this up!

Descriptions of several past Pentacom productions followed. One of them was a sitcom called *Que Pasa, USA*. There was also a documentary based on Tennessee Williams' last public reading in Key West at the former Sands Beach Club. Pentacom had done a documentary called *Son of a Son of a Sailor Man* which Shep described as a "madcap profile of Jimmy Buffet and his music."

If I was still with him, Shep wrote on the last page of his fax, we should talk — initially on the phone. For the next few days we kept missing each other, which was fine, friends advised. You don't want him to think you're too anxious, they said.

When Shep and I finally connected, I tried to envision how he might look from the sound of his voice. Tall, I imagined, and deeply tanned, with snowy white hair. No cigar. No ponytail. Shep sounded like a moderate sort of romantic. I saw him sprawled on a deck chair next to his pool, California languid, with a portable phone and a liter of mineral water chilling in a silver ice bucket.

"Are you negotiating with other producers right now?" Shep asked, when I finally got through to the coast. "Have you had many offers?"

"You're the first," I said.

Wrong answer, friends admonished later.

"He'll think you're easy!"

How many times have I heard that?

"We're swarming with offers," I was supposed to say. "I'm just trying to pick the right one, Shep."

Shep explained the process whereby he would turn my stories about Key West into a screenplay or sitcom. First he needed to check with some Hollywood friends and associates, find out if they liked the idea of *Postcards* as much as he did. Then, the option.

"We'll offer you some money, an amount so small it will shock you," Shep said. "We'll option your story, or your life, or your life's story. Something like that."

"Option the story of my life?" I asked.

"Yes," Shep said. "For six months or a year, while we work at